Spinning Through Clouds

Spinning Through Clouds
Tales from an Early Hoosier Aviator
by Max E. Knight

Indiana Historical Society Press
Indianapolis 2007

Printed in Canada

This book is a publication of the
Indiana Historical Society Press
450 West Ohio Street
Indianapolis, Indiana 46202-3269 USA
www.indianahistory.org
Telephone orders 1-800-447-1830
Fax orders 317-234-0562
Online orders @ shop.indianahistory.org

Photo credits for front cover: iStockphoto, iStock International Incorporated
(photo composite by Stacy Simmer)

The paper in this publication meets the minimum requirements of American National Standard for
Information Sciences—Permanence of paper for Printed Library materials, ANSI Z39.48-1984.

Library of Congress Cataloging-in-Publication Data

Knight, Max E., 1926-
  Spinning through clouds : tales of an early Hoosier aviator / by Max E. Knight.
     p. cm.
  Includes index.
  ISBN-13: 978-0-87195-256-1 (alk. paper)
1. Knight, Max E., 1926- 2. Air pilots—Indiana—Biography.
3. Aeronautics—Indiana—History. 4. Knight Airport—History. 5. Lynn
(Ind.)—History—20th century. I. Title.
  TL540.K575A3 2007
  629.13092—dc22
  [B]
                              2007039070

A publication from the Eli Lily Indiana History Book Fund

In memory of my longtime editor and great friend Jerry Davis,
who edited the first chapter of this book before suffering a fatal heart attack
at his Fishers, Indiana, home.

For those men and women who flew by the seat of their pants and made aviation history,
including my father, Clarence Knight, owner and operator of the Knight Airport at Lynn
in eastern Indiana from 1936 to 1941.

Contents

Introduction

Max Knight, the author of this book, virtually lived in the air from 1936 to 1941. Flying was as common to Max as riding in an automobile is to children today. Max's father, Clarence Knight, owned and operated an airport until being forced to close it only a few weeks prior to the start of World War II.

The airport was located on a gravel road two miles south and one mile east of Lynn, Indiana. Telephone poles along the north side of the field were shortened to five feet so the airplanes could land in the tiny twenty-acre field. The runway ran north and south, and with prevailing winds out of the southwest, the pilots soon learned to compensate for the constant crosswind. The poles that eventually brought electrical lines to the airport came through a field from the adjoining road north so they would not hinder the planes taking off or landing.

On weekends people flocked to the Knight Airport at Lynn and spent hours watching the planes as they flew in and out of the short field. Many took their first airplane ride, sometimes in an open cockpit capable of handling two people side by side. Others chose to fly in the closed cockpit of a Taylorcraft although only one passenger could go at a time. Dozens learned to fly at the airport as Myron (Nick) Nicholson gave flying lessons. Nick, from Richmond, Indiana, was nineteen years old when he first started as chief pilot for the airport. Lee Crossman, a veteran pilot from Muncie, later came on weekends to help when the load became too much for one pilot.

In the second year the field was in operation, Knight purchased farmland adjoining the airport and laid out an east-west runway. This greatly enhanced the safety of flying in and out of the airport.

During its five years of operation, the Lynn Airport became a focal point of the community as it grew from one Waco 10 biplane (an airplane with two fixed wings, one mounted above the other) to a total of eight aircraft stationed at the field. Knight first added a 40-horsepower Taylorcraft, then a newer 50-horsepower Taylorcraft, and finally a 65-horsepower Taylorcraft for teaching flying lessons. He also owned a Fairchild 24-CB. Other planes stationed at the Lynn Airport by area pilots included a Waco F, a Great Lakes Trainer, an Aeronca K, a Travel Air, and a Curtiss-Wright Pusher, whose owner split time between Lynn and the Nixon Airport west of Richmond.

Knight considered purchasing a J-3 Piper Cub instead of the Fairchild, especially after Indiana flying legend Lee Eikenberry came to the field to tout the bright yellow airplane.

Eikenberry was a sight to see in his salesman attire that included a fedora hat, white shirt, and dark suit with a colorful necktie. The J-3 he flew into the airport to show Knight was immaculate, and the sun sparkled off the shiny fabric. But the Lynn Airport owner preferred side-by-side seating instead of the tandem featured in the J-3, so he purchased the Fairchild.

The era prior to the start of World War II was a time when pilots learned to fly with little more than a compass for direction, an altimeter to measure altitude or distance from the earth, and an air speed indicator. The fuel gauge often consisted of a wire shaped like a 7 that descended into the tank in front of the windshield. Cross-country flying meant following a railroad to your destination. Railroads were easy to spot leaving any nearby town or city, and the compass told you the direction you were flying.

In October 1941, with war on the horizon, Knight received notice from the Indiana Civil Air Patrol that he would be required to make two scouting flights daily. He did not have the manpower to meet these new requirements, so on November 1, 1941, the airport closed.

Today the airport runway is a soybean field. It is doubtful whether the owner of the property knows that once upon a time there, aviation leaped forward in Indiana history with the roar of airplanes and the excitement of seat-of-your-pants flying.

CHAPTER ONE

Fate Steps In

If the engine of your plane burps, exit immediately.

Although this story takes the Knight Airport at Lynn, Indiana (the Lynn Airport), through its five years of flourishing as one of the biggest attractions in east central Indiana, the story actually begins eleven years earlier. In June 1925 Clarence Knight, Max Knight's father, purchased a Standard airplane of World War I vintage and had it delivered from Muncie, Indiana, to the farm home where he and his wife, Minnie, lived north of Lynn. Two men delivered the airplane on the bed of a truck. They hoisted the plane to the ground, fastened the wings in place, and crawled in the truck to leave.

"Wait!" Clarence shouted. "Who's going to teach me how to fly?"

"Don't know, Mister," came back the answer. "We just deliver. We ain't never flown one and ain't about to." With that they drove out of the field and headed home.

Clarence decided he had no choice but to learn on his own. Each day he had his friend Carl (Crackshot) Houser spun the propeller and fired up the engine. Then Clarence taxied the plane round and round the field, sometimes getting up enough speed for it to lift a foot or two off the ground. He did this for three weeks. When he was able to lift the plane ten to twelve feet off the surface before setting back down, his confidence rose to the point that he was ready for a solo attempt.

On the last day of June, Clarence walked into the kitchen of their home and said to his wife, "Minnie, I'm going to take it up. I've been practicing for three weeks and know I can do it."

Without even looking at him his wife muttered, "You'll kill yourself. Don't be stupid."

But Clarence was convinced and urged his wife to come with him to the field and watch his flight.

"I have no intention of watching you kill yourself," Minnie answered. "I'll wait right here until Crackshot comes in to tell me you have crashed."

Clarence, with a snort of disgust, headed out the door. He was picture perfect as a pilot with his white coveralls, white shoes, white spats, black helmet, and goggles trimmed in white. Crackshot was waiting at the plane as Clarence walked up.

"Let's get this over with," Clarence said to his friend as he climbed into the open cockpit. Crackshot walked to the front of the plane.

"Switch off!" Crackshot yelled.

"Switch off!" answered Clarence.

Photo of Clarence Knight moments before his plane, a Standard J-1 of World War I vintage, exploded.

Crackshot pulled the propeller through twice to prime the engine for starting.

"Switch on!" Crackshot called.

"Switch on!" came back the answer from the pilot.

"Contact!" yelled Crackshot.

"Contact!" Clarence answered.

Crackshot lifted his right leg in the air to get more leverage as he spun the propeller, and the engine started on the first pull. But as it started it backfired. A ball of fire came roaring out of the exhaust and onto the fuselage. Fortunately for Clarence he had not fastened his seat belt. He leaped out of the burning airplane, hit the ground, and rolled to a stop. In seconds the airplane was nothing but a black hulk of metal.

Clarence sobbed all the way to the house, Crackshot by his side. When he entered the kitchen door he said, "Minnie! Oh, Minnie! It caught fire and burned. I can't believe it. It's gone! Burned!"

Minnie, who stood an even five feet tall, put her arms around the waist of her six-foot-tall husband and said over and over, "Oh, Clarence, I am so sorry. I am so sorry. I am so sorry."

Crackshot was standing in the doorway. As he watched Minnie console her husband, he could see her face under Clarence's right arm. She was grinning from ear to ear.

HANGAR FLYING USA
The Standard J-1

The Standard airplane that was destroyed by fire before Clarence got it off the ground was a primary training aircraft from World War I. The airplane was used to teach young men how to fly but was never flown in combat. It had two open-cockpit seats in tandem and officially was known as the Standard J-1, manufactured by the Standard Aircraft Corporation of Elizabeth, New Jersey. The plane featured a 90-horsepower Hall-Scott A-7 engine with a carburetor off to one side that made it susceptible to fire.

The airplane was excellent for dual instruction as the pilot sat in the rear seat within reach of the student in the front open cockpit. Messages were passed back and forth by the instructor in a unique manner: The instructor would tap the student on the back of his head, generally using a short stick. The student would turn far enough around in his seat to grab the note and follow instructions. In today's world of electronics the method seems crude. But it worked.

Only 1,600 J-1 planes were built before production was halted due to the problem Clarence encountered as the engine was fired up for his solo flight. To solve the dilemma the Curtiss Aeroplane and Motor Company purchased more than 1,000 war surplus Standards, equipped them with its own 90-horsepower OX-5 engine, and named them the Standard-Curtiss J-1.

Pilots found the Standard-Curtiss J-1 perfect for barnstorming (in which pilots set their planes down in farm fields to offer rides to those in the area), aerial mapping, and photography. A barnstormer could land the J-1 in a small field and haul some sixty passengers during a normal day. The surge in automobile production called for more highways and aerial views and was a boost for the J-1. Mapping terrain from the air was far superior to shooting pictures from ground level. Another advantage of the plane was that after the market became saturated with aircraft in 1922, the J-1 could be purchased for $1,995, less than any comparable airplane on the market.

CHAPTER TWO

Nine-Year-Old Pilot

A good landing is one from which you can walk away.
A great landing is one in which you can fly the plane again.

On Monday, August 24, 1936, Max Knight took his first flying lesson in a J-2 Taylor Cub. He was nine years old at the time, one day shy of his tenth birthday. Later that day his father, Clarence Knight, informed Max that he had purchased an airplane and was going to start an airport at the family's farm south of Lynn, Indiana. The plane was a bright red 90-horsepower Waco 10 biplane with a Curtiss OX-5 engine. This is the story of how it all began and the fantastic five years that followed.

Two days before that tenth birthday Clarence asked Max if he would like to take a ride in an airplane. The answer was a resounding "Yes!" The two journeyed from Lynn to Rushville, Indiana, where Clarence had made arrangements with pilot L. B. (Tat) Lower to take them up. The airplane was a Waco F biplane, dark red with white striped markings on the fuselage, or the body portion of the airplane.

Tat, considered one of the best pilots in Indiana, gave Clarence and Max leather helmets—with goggles attached—to wear due to the strong wind that blew into the open cockpits. Tat also brought a leather cushion from his office for Max to sit on so he could see over the side. Clarence and Max crowded into the front cockpit—Clarence on the right, Max on the left.

The plane bounced and skipped as they headed down the runway and then lifted off so smoothly that Max caught his breath. In moments they were climbing at a fast, thrilling pace. Max was intrigued by the countryside below with its miniature-looking houses. He spotted a pickup truck speeding down a gravel country road, dust flying behind it. Max looked at his dad. Clarence had a big smile on his face. They gave each other the thumbs-up sign.

Tat leveled off at 1,000 feet and flew south from the airport. A river wandered southwestward; the sunlight sparkling off it made it look like a string of diamonds. In a field a team of horses stood hooked to a wagon, and two men pitched hay onto its bed. Cars and trucks looked like moving ants as they headed southeast along the paved state highway.

When the plane circled east and then back north, suddenly there to the left was the city of Rushville. The buildings looked like toys, and the courthouse tower appeared to be reaching for the sky.

They flew for what seemed to Max only a few short minutes but actually was almost a half hour before Tat returned to the airport, reduced the speed of the engine, and settled the Waco toward the runway. The landing was as smooth as cream on a bucket of milk. As they taxied to the hangar, Clarence and Max unhooked their seat belts and got on their knees on the seat to look back at Tat in the rear cockpit. They both gave him a thumbs-up sign and knew from that moment that flying was in their blood. Both father and son were hooked.

On the way home, riding in a pickup truck, Clarence told his son he was going to the Nixon Airport west of Richmond the next day to take a flying lesson. "How about you?" Clarence asked. "Want to give it a try?"

"Oh, yes! But can I?" Max said, a big but dubious smile on his face. "Gee, Dad, I'm only nine years old. Are you sure they'll let me take a flying lesson?"

"I don't know for sure," his father answered, "but I see no reason why not. Since your birthday is coming up, I'll make it a special present. If they say no, at least we tried."

Robert A. (Bob) McDaniels did not say no. In fact, he took two cushions from the small airport office, placed them in the rear seat of the J-2 Taylor Cub—one for Max's back and one for him to sit on—and told Max to climb aboard.

The J-2 was a lot smaller than the Waco Max had ridden in the day before, and the seat was quite narrow. Whereas the Waco had an open cockpit, the J-2 was closed. To get in the plane, Bob lifted a door upward instead of to the right or left as in an automobile. The two seats were tandem—one in front of the other—and to Max's surprise, Bob told him to get in the rear seat. It seemed more natural for the pilot to be in the rear and for the passenger to be up front, as in the Waco, but the instrument panel position dictated that the pilot sit in front.

Bob taxied the small yellow airplane to the northeast corner of the airport runway, turned into the southwest breeze, and shoved the throttle forward. In moments the plane was in the air.

The J-2 was controlled by a floor stick and two rudder bars or pedals, called by either name. Bob had Max take hold of the stick and feel the movement as he turned the plane right and left. He then had the young boy stretch his legs until he could touch the rudder bars, again feeling the movement as the pilot worked them both directions.

After letting Max get a feel of the stick and rudder bars, the pilot banked the plane to the east, and there in front of them was the city of Richmond. It looked huge compared to Rushville. The spires of three churches ascended high into the air, and a train slowly moved

This serene countryside was the center of flying activity for more than five years. The Lynn Airport hangar stood at the bottom of this photo with the Knight house two hundred feet northwest.

westward through town. The sight was overwhelming to Max. For a few moments he forgot why he was up there in the first place. Bob brought him back to business.

"Keep the nose level with the horizon," the pilot cautioned, yelling at Max from the front tandem seat, "and learn to listen for the sound of the engine. It will let you know if there is trouble or if you are going down or up. You must become a part of the airplane if you want to be a good pilot."

The instructor had Max move the stick forward so that the plane went into a shallow dive and then pull it back so that they climbed upward.

"I'm on the stick with you, so don't get scared," said Bob. "Now, push your left rudder slightly and move your stick to the left."

Max did as instructed, and the J-2 turned left. Max wanted to look down but was afraid to turn his head until the plane had once again leveled out.

"You're doing good!" the instructor yelled at Max. "Now do the same thing to the right. Easy! Don't override the right rudder. Good. Easy does it. I won't let you override, so relax."

Max realized that relaxing was vital but found instead that he was wound as tight as the strings in a baseball.

"Okay," Bob called out. "Let go and enjoy the ride back to the airport!"

The flying lesson was the shortest half hour of Max's life. When Bob landed and taxied back to the airport hangar, Max knew he must learn to fly. Little did he know the surprise his father had for him as they headed home to Lynn.

Back in the pickup truck Max bubbled over with excitement, telling his father how great the flying lesson was. Clarence quietly said, "I've got another surprise for you. Now don't tell your mother, but I bought an airplane. We are going to start an airport at Lynn, something I have wanted to do all my life. I bought a Waco 10 with an OX-5 engine from Bob McDaniels and hired a young man from Richmond named Nick Nicholson to fly it for us. The plane is open cockpit and similar to the one we rode in down at Rushville. I told Nick I would work all night if necessary to get the landing strip as smooth as possible and call him at the Richmond Airport when it is ready."

Max realized his mouth was hanging open in disbelief as he tried to absorb what his dad was saying. Their own airplane. Their own airport. And the only thing he could think to ask was, "What will Mom say?"

Later that evening Clarence got up the nerve to tell his wife, Minnie, and Max heard her yell from the kitchen, "What!"

But Clarence was persuasive, and reluctantly his wife agreed. She did not like the idea and told her husband he would bankrupt the family but agreed to give it a try and see what happened.

At dawn the next morning, Clarence was in the field that would become the airport runway, dragging large wooden posts behind his pickup truck, doing all he could to make the ground as smooth as possible. The dust rolled in banks as the truck went back and forth down the center of the twenty-acre field.

Clarence decided he needed a strip 150 feet wide, and with the wooden posts 8 feet in length, it took a lot of trips to cover the area. He did not quit for lunch, so Max took him a sandwich and Coke and then rode with his dad until midafternoon, when the new airport owner rolled to a stop where the hangar would be built.

"It's not perfect," he said to Max, "but for now, it will do. Nick shouldn't have any problems getting in with the Waco."

Clarence hurried to the house and made a phone call to the Richmond Airport. He turned to his wife and son and said, "Nick is ready to leave. He should be here in twenty minutes. Let's take a couple folding chairs and go over to the field to watch him come in."

The chairs were a good idea, but both Max and Clarence were too excited to sit down. Minnie did so, turning her chair so she could look southwest, the direction from which the plane would be arriving. All three strained their eyes looking to spot the Waco. Minnie saw it first. Although still not sure of her husband's sanity, Minnie pointed and said, "There it comes."

The sighting of that solid red airplane was the greatest moment of Max's young life.

Nick flew over the field, dipped his wings in greeting, banked left to line up with the north-south runway, and set the plane down with a cloud of dust in a perfect three-point landing, all the plane's wheels touching the ground at the same time. He taxied to where Clarence was standing and let the engine idle.

"Any problems?" Clarence yelled to his pilot.

"None," came back the answer. "This plane is as sweet as honey. You and Max ready to go up?"

Both chorused, "Yes!"

Clarence and Max climbed onto the wing and then into the two-passenger front seat. Father and son had already donned helmets in anticipation of the flight, and Max brought a pillow from the house to sit on. Once they were belted in, Clarence gave a thumbs-up to Nick, and the plane began to roll.

When Nick gave the plane full throttle, Max's head jerked back and bumped against the rear seat pad. He looked at his dad and then looked back over the side of the plane. They were about twenty feet off the ground and climbing. Chills ran down Max's spine. This was their airplane! He would be riding in it often, maybe even flying it!

Nick leveled off at 1,000 feet and circled over the town of Lynn. People on the street looked up at the plane, and Max felt proud. The tall water tower in the heart of town reminded him of a candle in the center of a cake. Max saw an ABC passenger bus pull into the Lynn station. As people alighted they looked skyward at the plane.

Since Max went to school at a small town east of Lynn named Spartanburg, Nick headed there before turning back toward the field. In doing so he followed the railroad east, and suddenly a train came into view—one of the most thrilling sights of Max's ten years on the earth. Smoke poured from the engine, and the freight cars rocked back and forth in a never-ending rhythm as the train chugged along. Max's eyes followed the red caboose until it disappeared out of view.

Max's school appeared to be the size of a tiny box as the plane reached 2,000 feet. The pond next to the school where he and his friends skated in winter looked like a dot of water in a landscape of trees. Max felt another chill go down his spine as Nick circled the small town and headed toward Clarence's runway.

As soon as the plane was on level flight, Nick, in the open cockpit rear seat, banged on the fuselage to get Clarence's attention. When he looked back, Nick motioned for Clarence to take the stick and fly the plane. Giving Nick another thumbs-up, Clarence took the controls, knowing Nick could grab the stick in the backseat if there was a problem. Clarence flew the plane for ten minutes or so. Then he let Max take over. The thrill of flying that plane was awesome.

After landing back on the runway, the Waco was tied down where the hangar later would be built so that no winds could damage it, and Clarence and Nick went to work on the field. The dust had to be brought under control, and the ruts of crops needed more smoothing out for safety. Many bags of road salt and many trips back and forth with the pickup truck pulling the posts finally got the field in shape. On Sunday afternoon, August 30, 1936, the Lynn Airport officially opened. The place was packed with people.

HANGAR FLYING USA
The Wright Brothers at Kitty Hawk

The Knight Airport at Lynn, Indiana, opened only thirty-three years after the world's first free, controlled, and sustained flight in a power-driven, heavier-than-air machine. This first flight was accomplished by Orville Wright in partnership with his brother Wilbur at Kitty Hawk, North Carolina, on December 17, 1903.

Wilbur Wright was born on April 16, 1867, two miles northeast of Millville, Indiana, in Henry County, only twenty miles southwest of what, in 1936, would become the Lynn Airport. Orville was born in 1871 about forty-five miles southeast of Lynn in Dayton, Ohio.

Wilbur, who died of typhoid fever at the age of forty-five, flipped a coin with his brother to see who would make the first flight. Wilbur won the coin toss, which took place on December 14, 1903. But during Wilbur's first attempted flight that day the plane was damaged. Three days later, after the repairs were made and the wind was right, Orville took off after 10:00 a.m. and flew a distance of 120 feet in twelve seconds.

Wilbur then got another turn, flying 175 feet, only to see his brother top that mark by 25 more feet on his second attempt. Wilbur finished the day with the longest flight, 852 feet in fifty-nine seconds. However, after landing a gust of wind caught the plane and turned it over, causing extensive damage.

Were it not for a steering problem on an earlier attempt at flight in an airplane built by Samuel Pierpont Langley, one might never have heard of the Wright brothers. On October 7, 1903, seventy-one days before the Kitty Hawk flight, pilot Charles Manly tried to take off in the Langley aircraft, only to find he could not steer it. As the machine reached flying speed, it veered off course and crashed. Langley Air Force Base, Hampton, Virginia, is named for this famous inventor.

Today the Wilbur Wright Birthplace and Museum, located near Millville, is one of the feature aviation attractions in the state of Indiana. A replica of the 1903 Wright Flyer is on display at the museum.

Wilbur Wright checks the wind velocity (speed) while brother Orville Wright looks on. This photo was taken in February 1909 in Paris, France.

CHAPTER THREE

Airplane Rides

*There are three rules for making a smooth landing.
Unfortunately, no one knows what they are.*

At the entrance to the airport driveway, Clarence erected a sign that said, "15 Minute Ride, Can Take Two at A Time, $1 each." On that first Sunday afternoon at the Knight Airport at Lynn, a line of people extended from the table where visitors signed in for rides to the gravel road north, a distance of 100 feet. There was no way everyone could get a ride before nightfall, but they all waited in anticipation. Surprisingly all but the final eight at the back of the line got their airplane ride before darkness closed down the first day of operation. Clarence gave each of those eight people a slip of paper with "free ride" written on it, and all returned at a later date.

Nick had a routine he followed for airplane rides. He flew south from the airport to the town of Fountain City, then north along U.S. 27 to Lynn, east to the little town of Crete, and then back to the airport. You could set your watch on fifteen minutes for the trip.

Upon landing several wanted to go a second time, but Clarence urged them to come back later so he could get as many as possible up that first day. Some also wanted to be flown over their homes, and again Clarence encouraged them to return later and this would be accomplished.

All in all, it was a great opening day.

Max was in charge of the soft-drink concession. Clarence had purchased a new galvanized tank (actually called a horse tank) and filled it with water and chunks of ice. He had to drive twelve miles to Richmond to purchase the ice in 50-pound blocks and had built an insulated wooden box to hold the ice in storage. Two blocks, purchased on Friday, sufficed for the weekend.

Max's thriving business sold Coke and lemon-lime and orange soda in six-ounce bottles for five cents each. On the weekends he always dressed like a pilot when operating his soft-drink stand, wearing a helmet with the goggles on top and a shirt his mother had sewn with "Knight Airport" on the back and "Max" above the front pocket.

Nick was a busy man taking passengers for rides on weekends through September. During the week Nick, Clarence, and a hired man, Ralph Polley, worked on the construction of a hangar for a Taylorcraft airplane to be delivered in the spring of 1937. This would give the airport a plane for teaching others how to fly.

On the first weekend in April 1937, Everett (Coxey) Cox, owner of the Winchester (Indiana) Airport and Taylorcraft salesman, landed at the Lynn Airport. He was flying a blue and red Taylorcraft with a 40-horsepower Continental engine. It was Clarence's new plane, and within the hour Coxey took Clarence and then Max for a ride. Both fell in love with the Taylorcraft, especially since the pilot and the occupant sat side by side in a closed cockpit, and it was flown with a steering wheel instead of a stick. It was a perfect plane for giving flying lessons.

Nick flew with Coxey back to Winchester and brought the plane home to Lynn. Clarence got in as soon as Nick taxied to a stop, and they were gone for an hour. During that time Nick wrung out the new airplane, spinning three turns from 6,000 feet, doing a wingover, and even ending with a loop, in which the airplane flies in a vertical circle, as he flew over the airport. The smiles on the faces of the two men when they taxied to a stop at the new hangar was a picture for life.

Max did not get his first chance at the controls of the new plane until the next day. Nick drove in from Richmond for lunch and then asked if Max would like to go with him to Muncie to check out licensing the Taylorcraft. It would be a routine check that took only twenty minutes to accomplish but was required by law. Max, of course, said yes.

As Nick leveled out the plane at 2,000 feet he told Max to take hold of the wheel and get the feel of its movement. Immediately Max put the plane into a shallow dive toward the ground, and when he pulled back on the wheel he pulled up into a stall (a sudden drop in altitude that occurs when an airplane's speed drops below that required to maintain flight). In panic Max looked at Nick, who was laughing.

"Easy, boy," he said to the ten-year-old. "Let the plane fly itself. You ease the controls to keep it level. Try again."

This time Max did better and in minutes had the plane on a level flight.

"Good," Nick called out above the engine noise. "Now put your feet on the rudder bars and get the feel as I move them right and left."

Concentrating on the rudder bars, Max forgot the wheel and in seconds was again in a power dive, descending quickly toward the ground.

"Bring it back level," Nick said, still not putting his hands on the wheel in front of him.

"Good," he said when Max had the plane level once more. "Now keep the nose on the horizon and get the feel of the rudder bars without concentrating on them."

Slowly the plane banked to the right as Max felt the rudder bar on his right foot maintain pressure. At the same time Max turned the wheel slightly right, and to his surprise the plane made a normal, slow turn.

"Okay, ease it back level," Nick said, and Max did as told with satisfying results. The plane now was level and headed directly for the airport at Muncie, a dot in the distance. Max turned it back over to Nick to land, but the elation he felt being in the new plane was impossible to describe.

Clarence was ready for Nick to give lessons to anyone who wanted to learn to fly. Word spread, and within two weeks Nick had given lessons to eight men and one woman. The airport was growing by leaps and bounds.

As for Max, he was in the air virtually every day that the weather was nice. By the summer of 1937 he had mastered the basics of flying.

Nick taught one lesson of confidence that had Max sweating before it ended. Nick had always kept his hands on the wheel while teaching Max how to land an airplane. It was vital in such a small field to sideslip the plane at the edge of the runway if you were coming in high. To sideslip, the wheel of the plane was turned to the right while the rudder was gently pushed left. This resulted in the plane going into a sideslipping mode where the plane lost some of its forward motion, quickly dropping toward the ground. Max tried several times before making his first landing with Nick carefully watching and his hand on the wheel for safety.

After landing the Taylorcraft a few times, Nick told Max to fly cross-country for a little while since there was nothing going on midweek at the airport. Max set a course for Muncie, back to Winchester, and then home.

Nick settled in his corner of the seat, laid his head against the side window, and apparently fell sound asleep. This was not unusual since on long flights the instructor often set the stabilizer to keep the plane level and dozed off while Max read comic books. He knew if there was a problem, Max would wake him up or tell him they were nearing their destination.

As Max headed south from Winchester, he glanced over at Nick, who had not moved. "So," Max thought, "why not land at the airport on my own? Nick won't know what is happening until the wheels touch the ground."

Max flew over the airport and saw the windsock with a breeze from the south, so he lined up on the runway north to south and cut back on the throttle. As he passed over the gravel road at the edge of the field, Max realized he was much too high to land, so he hit the throttle and went around again. Nick never moved, apparently sound asleep.

It took two more tries before Max got the plane low enough to correctly sideslip over the end of the runway. He felt the wheels touch the ground and saw the plane was midway down the field. The Taylorcraft bounced once and then settled like a feather, rolling to a stop well short of the fence at the end of the field.

As Max leaned back against the seat and gave a huge sigh of relief, he realized sweat was pouring off his forehead. He then glanced over at Nick. As he did, the instructor grinned and slowly turned his head to reveal he had had his left eye open all the time, making sure Max did not get in trouble.

That first landing on his own occurred the first week of July 1937, one month before Max's eleventh birthday. It was only one of many landings he would make during the next four years.

HANGAR FLYING USA
Homemade Aircraft

In the early years of flying a student pilot often soloed with only two or three hours of instruction. Many learned to fly in World War I planes and often purchased the planes in which they soloed. But some pilots, like Robert Retz, a native of Farmland, Indiana, did not have the money to buy a plane, so they built planes of their own.

Retz's story begins in 1927, when he and a friend departed for Kansas City to enroll in the aviation program at the Sweeney Aviation School. The school had a four-month course that taught engine mechanics, welding, stick and airframe construction, and rigging. Although flight training was offered, neither man had the funds to participate, so they returned to Farmland in the spring of 1928.

RANDOLPH COUNTY HISTORICAL MUSEUM

A week after returning home, Retz became friends with a barnstorming pilot and signed on with him as a mechanic. During that summer he got his first taste of flying and was hooked.

In August cowboy movie actor Ken Maynard, who was sport flying in the area, said he was looking for someone to serve as mechanic for his Travel Air biplane. Retz immediately told Maynard he was his man. The two hit it off, and a strong friendship resulted.

In 1929 Retz built his first airplane, a biplane with only one cockpit, featuring a four-cylinder Chevrolet engine adapted for light aircraft. He purchased a farm north of Farmland and opened his own airport late that summer.

The Farmland Airport flourished until 1937, when Retz and a student he was teaching were killed in a plane crash. The biplane had performed to perfection when suddenly it lost power as the two men approached the runway. The plane nosed into the ground a few hundred yards from the landing strip. The two men died instantly.

Robert Retz, pilot and owner of the Farmland Airport, stands in front of a Fleet biplane with wheel covers Retz made to dress up the aircraft.

CHAPTER FOUR

Seat-of-the-Pants Flying

Takeoffs are optional. Landings are mandatory.

With only one pilot and two airplanes at the Knight Airport at Lynn, Clarence needed help on the weekends, and Lee Crossman, a pilot from Muncie, agreed to fly. He gave the student lessons, freeing Nick to fly the Waco carrying passengers. If there was not a lesson to give, rides were offered in the Taylorcraft. However, these were not as popular as rides in the open-cockpit Waco where two people could ride at once because the Taylorcraft carried only one passenger.

During the week it was a different story. Several student pilots came to the airport after work, and Nick gave them a lesson before dark. During summer months, the airport seldom had a day when a lesson was not given. Several local people also came for rides on sunny summer evenings.

On the weekends, Max worked out a system beside his soda pop tank where purchasing a drink automatically placed the customer on a shorter waiting list for sightseeing flights. The idea worked. Many people parked their cars in the parking lot and, instead of telling Clarence they wanted to take a ride, headed for the sign-in board next to the ice-filled tank. They spent five cents for a soda and cut short their waiting time. It was great for business.

On one Saturday in early June Nick had taken twelve couples for rides in the Waco when he stopped to fill up with fuel. This was Clarence's job, pouring the gasoline from two five-gallon cans into the plane's tank while standing on a stepladder. It was precarious work. Max waited at the foot of the stepladder to return the empty cans to a rack in the overhead gasoline tank south of the hangar while friend Paul Stout took care of the soft-drink business.

Clarence finished one can and as he reached for the second one, slipped and banged the empty can against the plane's engine. Nothing appeared to be damaged, so he poured in the second can and handed the empties back to his son before descending the ladder. When Max and Clarence were clear, Nick fired up the Waco and headed out with two more passengers.

The couple, a man and his wife, lived two miles southwest of the airport, and they asked Nick to fly over their home. Clarence got an extra fifty cents apiece for this, and Nick readily agreed.

As Nick lifted off the field he suddenly realized he had no power. Something was drastically wrong. The throttle was wide open, but the plane mushed into the air and cleared the fence at the end of the field by inches. Directly ahead, a half mile away, was a huge tree. Nick eased the plane to the right, missing the tree by less than ten feet.

The pilot knew he had to get back and land as quickly as possible. With the plane level he decided to turn left since that would get him back without any worry about electrical power lines. To the west was U.S. 27, and power lines went all the way from Lynn to Fountain City following a secondary road.

But when he eased the stick left, the plane lost even more power, and he quickly brought it back level. He had no choice. He knew he would crash if he tried to turn left. So he eased the stick right, and the power held although greatly diminished. Slowly the plane turned, missing another tree by a few feet. Directly ahead were the power lines bordering U.S. 27, and the pilot saw he would clear them by at least twenty feet so he continued his slow turn.

Nick glanced forward and realized the man in the front cockpit with his wife was pointing downward and looking back at him with a big smile on his face. Nick quickly glanced over the side and saw they were less than fifty feet over the top of the couple's farm home.

Nick did a quick wave to the man and continued his slow turn, the plane dropping lower each minute. Nick knew he had to clear those lines a second time on his approach, and now the plane was virtually hedge hopping over trees and going slower and slower.

As Nick saw the highway power lines directly ahead, he knew he had to go under them. He had no idea whether he could do it. At that moment he saw a field slightly to his right with no fence, so he eased the plane to that hole. Under the power lines went the Waco, missing them by inches.

In moments Nick landed safely at the airport. He was drenched in perspiration as he slowly taxied the airplane to the hangar. Clarence, Max, and several other men ran out as the plane stopped and Nick cut the engine. When Nick pushed himself up onto the back of the cockpit, Marion (Curly) Kennedy, one of the pilots who frequented the airport and was a mechanic at a nearby Chevrolet garage, set a stepladder against the engine and hurried up it. He took one look and yelled, "Nick, you got a magneto wire hanging loose." Apparently, when the gasoline can accidentally banged against the engine it had hit the wire and knocked it loose, resulting in a loss of power in the engine.

"Clarence," Nick said with a big sigh, "there's no way in the world I could make that flight and not crash. I had no power and had to go under the power lines down on the highway as I came around. That's an experience I do not ever want to repeat."

At that moment the couple in the front seat stood up. Both were smiling, and the farmer said to Clarence, "We went right over our house and could even see the chickens in the barnyard. That was wonderful. Here's three more dollars. Let's do it again!"

EUGENE (BUS) STEGALL AVIATION COLLECTION, MORRISSON-REEVES LIBRARY

1929 Waco 10 owned by Clarence Knight and photographed at Muncie, Indiana, Airport in 1939.

HANGAR FLYING USA
The Twin Beech

Two people, one pilot, open cockpits! As Max flew in later years, his thoughts often returned to the seat-of-your-pants flying that laid the groundwork for planes of the future. A pilot never relaxed completely while flying those early death traps for fear the unexpected might happen—and often did.

In 1937 the world of aviation took a tremendous leap forward. One of the prime moves was the introduction of the Beechcraft Model 18 or Twin Beech. It featured two 450-horsepower Pratt and Whitney Wasp Jr. engines. While there was no American market initially, the plane sold heavily in Canada and elsewhere. In the United States it gradually became popular for business executives.

The Twin Beech turned out to be the largest airplane Max had the privilege of flying throughout his career. The twin-engine, low-wing monoplane was of all-metal construction, with a single set of wings mounted below the body of the plane. It could handle a pilot, copilot, and six passengers. Max was amazed at the smoothness of the Pratt and Whitney R-985 engines.

Military versions of the Twin Beech were produced in the late 1930s. During World War II different versions of the plane were used by the Army Air Corps, the Navy, and the Army Air Force, which used them as air transports and for aerial photography.

Max said, "After learning to fly in a 40-horsepower Taylorcraft and spending many hours in an open-cockpit Waco with a 90-horsepower engine, feeling the power of those twin Pratt and Whitney engines sends chills down my spine even today. I never had the opportunity to fly a jet aircraft, but I can imagine the difference between the cumbersome early planes and the Twin Beech would be comparable to, say, the difference between a cargo plane and a Lear Jet."

A Twin Beech, similar to the one pictured here, was the largest plane Max flew in his years as a pilot (1936–79).

CHAPTER FIVE

The Flying Farmer

Parachutes are not necessary, but that first step is a big one.

The busy first weekend of June 1937 had ended, and Clarence was relaxing in his favorite steel-framed chair when the telephone rang. To his surprise the caller was Clyde Shockley, manager of the Muncie Airport.

"Clarence," said Clyde, known far and wide as the "Flying Farmer from Kokomo," "I've been hearing good things about your new airport and wondered if you would like to come over to Muncie tomorrow for lunch, my treat, so we can get acquainted?"

Clarence readily accepted the invitation and asked the veteran pilot if he objected to Max riding along. "Of course not," Clyde answered. "Happy to have him."

Since the Knight Airport at Lynn was on a dusty gravel road, Clarence and Max stopped at a friend's home in Lynn, borrowed a bucket of water, and washed the red pickup truck. "Gotta make a good impression," Clarence said as they drove away.

Clyde was waiting when Clarence and Max arrived at the airport's Spin Inn Restaurant. Max ordered a hamburger while Clarence had a late breakfast of ham and eggs. Clyde said he was a soup eater and ordered potato soup.

"Tell me about your airport," Clyde said, blowing on his soup to cool it enough to eat.

"Well," said Clarence, "I own two planes, a Waco 10 with an OX-5 engine for passenger rides and a 40-horsepower Taylorcraft for lessons."

Clyde grinned, blew on his soup again, and said, "If there's a better plane than a Waco I don't know what it is. The one I own has a Kinner B-5, 100-horsepower engine, and you couldn't buy it from me if I couldn't get another one. Did you buy the Taylorcraft from Coxey over at Winchester?" Clyde was referring to Everett (Coxey) Cox, distributor for the Taylor Aircraft Corporation of Alliance, Ohio, and owner of the Winchester Airport.

"Sure did," Clarence answered. "Coxey gave me a good deal so I could get started. I only paid $600 for the Taylorcraft, and it had less than one hundred hours logged. I got the Waco for $400, so actually I don't have a large investment in getting started."

The two men talked about the need for promoting aviation in Indiana. Clyde said, "Most of the small airports like Wall Field here in Muncie and Silver Fox over near Anderson have closed due to competition, not only from this airport but also from the bigger fields at Indianapolis and Fort Wayne. I'm not sure we could make it if we didn't have a contract with the Ball Brothers Company here in Muncie to haul freight. We do haul a lot of passengers on the weekends, but our pilot training is not what it should be. What's your strongest point?"

"For a small field," said Clarence, "we feel fortunate to have seventeen men and one woman signed up for flight instruction. And we are kept busy on weekends, like you, hauling passengers."

"Do you have a full-time instructor?" Clyde asked.

"Sure do," Clarence answered, "and he's a good one. His name is Myron Nicholson. He keeps the Taylorcraft busy evenings and weekends giving lessons and takes passengers in the Waco when he is free to do so. You know Lee Crossman here at Muncie? He comes over most weekends to help Nick, and a couple of pilots from the Nixon Airport at Richmond also pitch in when needed."

"Do you fly the planes?" Clyde asked.

"Yes and no," Clarence answered with a grin. "My one promise to my wife in opening the airport was I would never learn to land a plane, so no fear of my flying one into the ground. Come to think of it, I remember hearing a story about you and a hog. Any truth to the tale?"

Clyde leaned back, put his feet up on a nearby chair, and said, "That was one of my dumb mistakes, and it almost cost me my life. I bought a World War I Jenny over at Indianapolis and flew it up to Kokomo to show my wife. I landed okay, but as I was taking off in my pasture field I forgot I had hogs out there. I was halfway down the field when out of the corner of my eye I saw this huge sow running across my path. Need I say more? There was not enough of that Jenny left to pick up in a bucket."

"I also heard you took an unexpected parachute jump," Clarence said.

"Another dumb trick," said Clyde. "I had my Waco strung with fireworks and was going to put on a show for a local country club. It went fine until I pulled the third rope and blew off half my right wing. Fortunately I had put on a parachute, something I seldom do. So I rolled the Waco on her back, unbuckled my seat belt, and fell out. The parachute opened, and I landed safely, watching my beautiful Waco crash and burn off to my left. One funny thing did happen. As I walked through the country club gate carrying my parachute over my shoulder, one of the men thought I was a ghost. Come to think of it," Clyde said with a laugh, "I darn near was!"

The Muncie pilot pushed back his chair, got to his feet, and said, "Well Clarence, we've done a lot of talking. How about going for a spin over our fair city?" Max urged his dad to go, and in moments Clyde was heading his Waco into the wind and lifting off.

From that day Clarence and Clyde Shockley were aviation friends. A parting suggestion by the Muncie pilot proved to be a boost for the Lynn field. Clyde suggested that Clarence contact pilots in the area and invite them to station their planes at the Lynn Airport.

"Out in the country, on a gravel road, you can offer them tie-downs for a lot less than I can here in Muncie. Give it a try."

Clarence did as suggested. Soon eight planes were operating out of the Lynn field in addition to the two he owned.

The Flying Farmer dropped in at the Lynn Airport on three occasions, always during midweek when he was not busy at Muncie. He joined a long list of pilots who were instructed to buzz the house chimney before landing to let someone know a visitor was heading into the airport. Pilots delighted in seeing how close they could come to the top of the house. During the years the airport was in operation, that chimney became famous, especially after the newspaper at Muncie heard about it from Clyde and shot a picture through the front window of a diving airplane flown by the Muncie pilot.

Clyde Shockley was known as the "Flying Farmer." He managed the Muncie (Indiana) Aviation Corporation.

HANGAR FLYING USA
First Licensed Hoosier Pilot

Indiana pilots hold a special place in the history of aviation. None was more highly respected than the Hoosier State's first licensed pilot, Roderick Wright. Wright was born on a farm in Daviess County and attended Purdue University.

Wright caught the flying bug by reading everything he could find on pioneers Wilbur and Orville Wright. In June 1911 Roderick Wright attended an air exhibition in Evansville, Indiana, and decided he must become a pilot. He enrolled at the flight school operated by the Wright brothers at Dayton, Ohio.

On July 26, 1913, Roderick Wright earned his pilot's license and was given the number 254. This number from the international group called Federation Aeronautique Internationale designated him the first licensed pilot in Indiana. This international organization later was dropped from the United States registry and replaced by the United States Federal Aviation Agency in 1926 and the Federal Aviation Administration in 1958.

Wright was a master of many skills. He was a mechanic, test pilot, flight instructor, pilot for hauling passengers, and also a pilot for flying freight.

In 1933 Wright returned to his farm in Daviess County, bought an airplane, and built a private airfield and hangar. Several in the community, including most of his family, were taught to fly by Wright at this small airport.

On the list of other well-known Indiana pilots, the "Flying Irishman," Mike Murphy, is at the top. Murphy learned to fly in 1928. After soloing he purchased a JN-4 Jenny biplane and went barnstorming. Murphy was a daredevil. One of his featured acts was precision takeoff and landing from a small platform on the back of a fast-moving truck.

Murphy was a glider pilot during World War II. He crash-landed on D-Day and broke both legs. He was rescued and spent six months recovering. After the war he headed the Marathon Oil air fleet. He maintained an interest in aerobatics and stunt flying and acted as a judge in international competitions. Murphy died in 1981.

INDIANA'S EARLY BIRD PILOT

Roderick M. Wright (1887 - 1960), one of Indiana's first pilots, received Federation Aeronautique Internationale pilot license No. 254 in 1913. Member of Early Birds, a national group of pilots who flew solo between 1903 and 1916. He was a flight instructor and a test, charter, and cargo pilot. Served in Indiana General Assembly, 1953 - 1957.

ERECTED 1997 INDIANA HISTORICAL BUREAU AND CHILDREN AND GRANDCHILDREN OF DAVIESS COUNTY NATIVE RODERICK M. WRIGHT

Roderick Wright was a member of the Early Birds of Aviation, having flown between the years 1903 and 1916. No relation to the Wright brothers, Roderick learned to fly at the Wright School of Aviation in Dayton, Ohio.

CHAPTER SIX

Barnstorming

If you land in a cow pasture, be sure the cows are in the barn being milked.

Max was fast asleep when he felt his bed being shaken. He quickly woke up and realized Clarence was doing the shaking.

"I don't want your mother worrying about us, so I told her we are flying down to visit with Tat Lower at Rushville. But you need to know in case we have trouble. Actually, Nick and I are going barnstorming. We are going to a small town west of Cincinnati and will stop at Rushville on the way."

Clarence had talked barnstorming quite often since visiting with Clyde Shockley, knowing Clyde had made good money traveling the countryside to take people flying. Airplanes were an oddity to most rural people, and the chance to take a ride in one was virtually out of the question. You simply did not travel miles to an airport for recreation. Even though the Great Depression was ending, money remained a luxury few enjoyed. So barnstormers—pilots who set their planes down in farm fields to offer rides to those in the area—became a welcome attraction in the early years of aviation.

It is easily forgotten that in 1937, when Clarence and Nick left for their day of barnstorming, only ten years had passed since Charles Lindbergh made his solo flight from New York to Paris in a single-engine monoplane. If an airplane flew over a rural home, it was common practice to hurry outside to get a view of it. If the plane happened to be a trimotor, with three engines, it was the talk of the community for days.

Max quickly dressed and hurried over to the airport hangar where Nick was warming up the Waco. Both men wore helmets with goggles attached and carried jackets in case the weather turned bad. But as they taxied to the end of the runway, turned south, and roared down the field, the June day could not have been more perfect. Bright sun and wispy clouds were the order of the day. In moments the plane was out of sight headed southwest.

Clarence and Nick did stop at the Rushville Airport and have a cup of coffee with Tat (L. B. Lower) before heading onward. Tat had barnstormed several times, so he had words of advice for the two first-time barnstormers.

"Since the town where you are going is along the Ohio River," said Tat, "look for a level area next to the river but as close to the town as possible. Spring flood areas often make good landing strips when they are dry. Your bright red airplane is good since it really will shine on a day like this. Also, circle the town several times but do not do excessive aerobatics. You want the people to take rides in the plane, and aerobatics can scare them off."

After bidding Tat good-bye, Clarence and Nick headed south from Rushville and searched out each town name on top of either the depot or fire station to make sure they were on the right path. Nick flew at 1,000 feet, and some thirty minutes after leaving Tat, they could see the Ohio River in the distance. When they reached the river, Nick turned west and within a few minutes spotted the town where they were headed.

Nick descended to 200 feet and chose a perfect landing area between the town and the river. But to be safe Nick dropped down to treetop height to make sure nothing was in the field and was satisfied it was the place to land.

With the landing field secured, they climbed again to 200 feet, circled the town, and watched as people came out of houses and stores. Some people even parked their cars and got out to watch the bright red plane fly overhead. Clarence had printed leaflets ready as they flew directly down Main Street. He tossed them out a dozen or so at a time. The leaflets said, "Come fly with Clarence and Nick. Cost $1 per person, two passengers at a time. See your home from the air."

People rushed out to pick up the leaflets, and after flying back north over the same street Nick and Clarence headed for the landing strip. Nick had not even taxied to a stop before dozens of people came either running into the field or driving their cars to the gate and then hurrying to where the plane stopped. They quickly formed a line, so Clarence hurried to the first two who were waiting, collected their two dollars, and sent them on their way. Many in the line already had dollar bills in their hands, and Clarence knew they were in for a good day.

At that moment Clarence noticed two boys standing a little way off from the line of people. Both wore ragged overalls and were barefoot. Their hands were shoved deep into their pockets. Clarence knew they did not have a dime between them, so he motioned them to come over to where he was selling tickets.

"Guys," said Clarence, "would you like to take a flight?"

"Sure would," the older of the two answered, "but we ain't got no money."

"Tell you what," Clarence said, reaching into his pocket, "you take these two dollars, go to a filling station, and get me four cans of gasoline. Bring them to me, and I'll see you both get a free ride."

The boys looked at each other and then broke into big smiles. They grabbed the two dollars from Clarence, and off they went at full speed. A half hour later they were back, each carrying two cans. They handed Clarence his change. Those two boys got the longest flight of the day.

With the rides being ten minutes in length they were able to make five flights per hour, taking two at a time and bringing in ten dollars. Clarence and Nick were at the field a little more than six hours and, even with the free ride for the boys, collected seventy dollars. That was a huge amount of money in that era, and their expenses for the day were less than ten dollars.

All in all the day could not have gone better. Around the kitchen table that night Clarence gave a running account of the barnstorming experience. He had to do some fast talking to pacify Minnie, however. He kept saying to her, "I said we would visit Tat Lower, and we did." She still thought it wasn't necessary to risk two men and the plane on some "foolhardy shenanigans," so Clarence promised he would not do it again.

To Max, barnstorming was for heroes. He had heard the barnstorming tales from Clyde Shockley and read about the barnstorming exploits of great pilots from Jimmy Doolittle to Charles Lindbergh. Having his Dad and Nick join this elite group resulted in hero worship for the ten-year-old. He dreamed of the day when he, too, could be so daring.

HANGAR FLYING USA
Stunt Flying

There was only one way most pilots could afford an airplane after World War I—go barnstorming! Many pilots who later became famous followed this pattern, including Jimmy Doolittle and Florence (Pancho) Barnes. Doolittle went on to become a general in the Air Corps. Barnes became known worldwide for her Pancho Barnes Mystery Circus of the Air.

Barnstorming dates to the early days of American theater. Traveling acting companies went from town to town, seldom finding a legitimate theater building in which to perform. With no building available, the performances were held in barns. From this, actors became known as barnstormers.

Pilots landing at small towns to take passengers for rides seldom found an airport from which to operate. They would swoop low over barns as they landed in a cow pasture, hence the borrowing of the name barnstormers.

A good barnstorming pilot could haul from sixty to eighty passengers in a single day, charging one dollar per head. Expenses were minimal, meaning it was not unusual to clear fifty to sixty dollars, a big wage during that time.

Often a barnstorming pilot put on weekend shows of daredevil flying. One of the most popular events was wing-walking, a stunt in which a man or woman was fastened to a harness on the top wing of a biplane while the pilot did all kinds of maneuvers.

Even today this trick is still popular at flying events such as the annual Vectren Dayton Air Show held each summer at the Dayton (Ohio) International Airport. This show features acts such as the world-famous precision Air Force Thunderbirds, the next generation in fighter aircraft such as the F/A-22 Raptor and the F-117 Stealth bomber, and many antique aircraft, including a 1940 Waco biplane. These planes are not only on display but also participate in flying exhibitions.

Pilot Jim Franklin was considered one of the best at his trade—known for a wing-walking stunt he performed with his son, Kyle. He played all the big air shows until his death in a tragic accident when two planes collided in an air show in July 2005.

Jimmy Doolittle prepares for takeoff in a Curtiss military airplane at the Wright Airport at Dayton, Ohio.

CHAPTER SEVEN

Hedge Hopping

If you push the stick forward, the houses get bigger.
If you pull the stick back, they get smaller.

A fun but dangerous sport in the early days of flying was called hedge hopping. An airplane would fly almost at ground level, hopping over objects and scaring the daylights out of anyone caught unawares.

One favorite hedge-hopping target was the railroad. It was not unusual to see a conductor or brakeman walking along the tops of freight cars as a train slowly moved across the terrain. The pilot would drop down to the level of the train and force the man to fall flat against the top of the freight car, generally shaking his fist at the grinning fliers as they passed overhead. It was imperative the plane stay at hedge-hopping level until it was out of view of the people on the train so that none of them could read the identification number on the airplane.

Max was flying with his cousin Bud Knight from Danville, Illinois, when he spotted his friend Bill Green on top of a wagonload of hay, forking it level as another man tossed pitchfork loads to him. With a laugh Max said, "Get ready to jump, Bill!" and the plane dropped down to ground level. Sure enough, although it cleared the wagon by thirty feet, Green slid to the ground, not taking a chance. Max circled the field and saw Green shaking his fist at him as the pilot dipped his wings back and forth in greeting.

But Green got even with Max. The farmer also drove what then was known as a huckster wagon. This was a truck loaded with grocery and hardware items that stopped at homes and made it easy for housewives or farmers to purchase items without driving to town. Green's route called for him to be at the Knight property on Thursday afternoon.

Max saw the huckster wagon coming and went out to greet Green.

"Bill," he said, "I'm sorry I knocked you off that load of hay, but when I saw you there I couldn't pass up the opportunity. I hope you didn't hurt yourself."

"Nah," answered the huckster wagon driver, "I saw you with that big smile as you pulled up."

"Tell you what," Max said, "if you'll come over Saturday I'll have Nick take you for a ride over your farm."

"No thanks," came back the answer. "If God wanted man to fly he would have given him wings. I'm happy right where I am. But no hard feelings." Green reached under the left side counter of the wagon, pulled out a candy bar, and handed it to Max. "Here," he said with a grin, "this is on me."

"Gee, thanks," said Max, taking the candy bar. "I'm glad you're not mad at me."

The huckster wagon owned by Bill Green probably looked a great deal like the truck pictured here. This photo was taken in the 1920s in Terre Haute, Indiana.

Minnie arrived at that moment, so Max climbed down out of the wagon, peeling the paper off his candy bar as he did so. The chocolate bar looked delicious, and he took a big bite. Immediately, he thought the top of his head was going to explode.

Green had spent quite some time the evening before working red pepper into a small hole in the candy bar until the inside was almost solid with the fiery substance. Max had tears in his eyes for an hour. As for Green, he laughed so hard he finally had to sit down on the tailgate of the huckster wagon to catch his breath.

Max also got in trouble while hedge hopping two other times. On one occasion Max and Lee Crossman were flying when Max saw the father of a school classmate walking across his pasture field, herding his cattle in for milking. "That's Bill Hylton's dad," Max yelled at Lee. "Bill's in my class at school. Let's buzz him!"

Max dropped the plane down to fifty feet off the ground and flew directly over the top of the farmer. He then pulled the plane up and to the left. When Max looked back, Hylton's dad was shaking his fist at him. Max waved and flew on to the airport.

As Max and Lee landed and taxied toward the hangar, a pickup truck came barreling in from the east, dust rolling behind it. The truck skidded as it turned into the airport driveway and came to a stop. Hylton jumped out. Max knew he was in trouble.

Clarence realized immediately what had happened. He finally got Hylton calmed down but not before he threatened to have Max arrested. Hylton told Clarence that Max had caused his cows to run and would ruin their milk production. Clarence offered to take him for a ride to help ease the situation, but the farmer bellowed a loud, "No way!" The issue finally was settled when Clarence offered Hylton ten dollars to forget the whole thing, and the farmer reluctantly accepted.

A surprising development came from the incident. The classmate, Bill Hylton, later took his first airplane ride at the Knight Airport at Lynn. He went on to get his pilot's license and flew for many years.

The favorite hedge-hopping area for pilots from the airport was between Lynn and Fountain City on U.S. 27. For a distance of three miles the electrical lines followed the old U.S. 27 route west of the highway, meaning there were no obstructions in that stretch of new road.

A pilot would see an automobile or truck heading south on the highway, get in a straight line behind it, and then zoom over the top of the vehicle, missing it by a few feet and scaring the daylights out of the driver. It happened many times.

On another occasion Max again was flying, this time with a cousin from Muncie, Bud MacDonald. The lone automobile on the stretch of highway was moving at a slow pace, and Max told his cousin to hang on for some fun.

He leveled the Taylorcraft above the highway, pushed the wheel forward, and dove at the automobile, zooming over the top of it and up to the right. At that moment he looked back and saw the stripe down the side of the car—an Indiana State trooper.

As Max hurriedly turned toward the landing field, he saw the patrol car make a U-turn on the highway and head north. He knew it was streaking for the airport, so he quickly headed that way in hopes of landing and getting out of the plane before the trooper arrived.

As Max taxied to a stop, the trooper and Clarence were standing by the hangar waiting.

"Which one of you was flying that plane?" the trooper demanded. Since Max's cousin was twenty years old and Max was only fourteen, the trooper looked at Bud.

"He was," Bud said, nodding toward Max.

Max was petrified. He could see himself taking years to pay off a big fine, never flying again, and even worse, being hauled off to jail.

The trooper started at his toes and chewed out Max all the way to his head. Then he continued back down until he again reached his toes. Clarence did not say a word, knowing he might be facing a big fine for one of his planes endangering the life of a driver; it could even result in the field being shut down for a period of time.

"Sir," said Clarence, "I'm the owner of the airport, and this is my son. We all know we shouldn't hedge hop, but we all do it. Have you ever been up in an airplane?"

"No," the trooper answered. "And if all pilots fly like your son I am not sure I want to go up."

Clarence glanced at his son and saw he was as white as a whitewashed fence.

"Sir," Clarence again addressed the trooper, "if you haven't been up you've missed a great thrill. Would you object if Nick took you for a ride?"

Clarence was grabbing at straws to keep the trooper from writing a ticket or informing the Civil Aeronautics Authority (CAA) of the incident.

The trooper, who said his nickname was Red, walked around the Taylorcraft and then said, "Okay. I've thought for ages I should go to the Nixon Airport at Richmond and take flying lessons. But I've been so busy I haven't had time. Yes, I'd like to take a ride. But don't think, young man," turning to Max, "this gets you off the hook."

"Nick," said Clarence, "take this fine gentleman for a long ride."

Not only did Nick take Red for a half-hour ride, including flying over the trooper's home near Richmond, but he also had him take hold of the wheel while in flight. When they landed Clarence was waiting.

"Son," said Clarence, being more informal, "how would you like to learn how to fly, and it won't cost you a penny?"

Red accepted Clarence's offer to an extent. He did learn how to fly, but he paid for his lessons like anyone else. Red became a regular at the airport in his off-duty hours, soloed, and turned out to be an excellent pilot.

The following spring Max and Red were flying the Taylorcraft, first to Winchester, over to Muncie, and then back to Lynn. As they headed south over U.S. 27, Red was flying. The day was picture perfect.

When they reached the spot where Red should have turned the plane left to line up for a landing, he continued on down the new highway. There, in front of the plane, was a pickup truck, slowly moving south without a care in the world.

Red looked over at Max and said with a big grin, "Watch." With that he zoomed low over the unsuspecting driver of the truck, pulled up to the right, looked back, and said, still grinning, "You didn't see me do that!"

HANGAR FLYING USA
Doolittle's World War II Raid

Pulling crazy stunts with an airplane was not limited to pilots of Wacos, Jennies, Cubs, or, even Clarence's favorite, Taylorcrafts. One of the greatest feats of flying came during World War II when Lieutenant Colonel James Doolittle (aka Jimmy Doolittle of air-racing fame) led sixteen planes on a low-altitude raid of the Japanese homeland. The secret raid, known as the "Tokyo project," was launched in retaliation for the Japanese attack on Pearl Harbor. Its successful completion proved that Japan was vulnerable to attack.

Placed in charge of the mission by General Henry Arnold, Doolittle chose the B-25B, known far and wide as the "Mitchell," as the plane for the task. The Mitchell was a medium bomber considered highly versatile although extremely noisy. It featured two 1700-horsepower Wright R-2600 engines and would have a range of 2,500 miles with the extra fuel tanks the military planned on adding to each plane.

Twenty-four B-25s with five-men crews for sixteen of the planes were placed under Doolittle's command. While the crews were being trained, told only that the mission would be secret and extremely dangerous, modifications were made on the planes to make them lighter and to add as much fuel as possible to each. Then crews and planes were loaded aboard the aircraft carrier, the USS Hornet. *Several hours after setting sail in the Pacific Ocean, the Raiders were finally told the details of their mission.*

A chance encounter with a Japanese patrol boat forced the raid to be launched one day early. On April 18, 1942, Doolittle and his crew led the crews of the other fifteen bombers on their mission. In order to accomplish the raid, Doolittle and the other pilots had to perform several risky maneuvers. First, each pilot had to take off from a carrier deck, a feat that none had performed before. This accomplished, the bombers had to be flown approximately 650 miles, in single file, barely above the ocean in order to avoid detection by the Japanese. Doolittle and the other pilots managed this, too. The Raiders successfully hit targets in Tokyo and six other Japanese cities. Then, they headed for China, low on fuel and with night falling.

One plane landed in Siberia, where the crew was captured. The other fifteen planes were crash-landed, and the crews on these planes parachuted out. Unfortunately, three crewmen died while landing, and eight were taken prisoner by the Japanese. Three of the latter were executed, and one died in prison. The remaining members of Doolittle's Raid, sixty-four men from a total of eighty, made it safely to China. The five men in Russia escaped safely the following year, and four of the men held by the Japanese were released at the end of the war.

Ironically, Doolittle thought the mission was a failure. Instead, he and his men were considered heroes. After the sobering disaster at Pearl Harbor, Doolittle's Raid lifted American spirits considerably—at home and on the many fields of battle. The Raiders received honors and awards from both the U.S. and Chinese governments. Doolittle was promoted to general and awarded the Congressional Medal of Honor.

Captain Earl Light, Max's cousin, stands in front of the B-25 he often flew over the Knight homestead.

CHAPTER EIGHT

Ground Fog Danger

The only time you have too much fuel is when the plane is on fire.

A woman pilot from Richmond kept her Aeronca K airplane at the Knight Airport at Lynn, and she needed a part for the engine. Clarence instructed Nick to fly to the Aeronca factory at Middletown, Ohio, and get what was needed. Nick asked Max to go along.

It was a beautiful spring day as the two followed the railroad southeast toward the Ohio city. On cross-country flights, highways all look alike and often go off in different directions. Railroads were easy to follow, and these became the flight pattern for pilots in the years before radios and radar.

Cornfields were showing green and hayfields were waving in the wind as Nick settled in for the seventy-mile flight. Directly ahead a train weaved its way toward Cincinnati, looking like a long, dark, crawling serpent. Smoke billowed from the two steam engines pulling the train, and walking atop the third car from the front was the conductor. He would not see any shenanigans from the pilots today, as retrieving the part from the Aeronca plant was the goal, not hedge hopping.

Nick usually set the stabilizer on a cross-country flight so he could nod off to sleep, and Max got out his stack of ten-cent comic books to read. But on the flight to Middletown, both watched the scenery as they flew, and in less than an hour the airport for the Aeronca factory came into view.

Max looked at the altimeter as they were landing. He was surprised to find Middletown 500 feet lower than the elevation at Lynn even though the Aeronca factory, located near the city, was surrounded by hills on three sides.

As Nick headed for the main hangar to secure the needed part, Max got out of the plane and sat in the shade of the wing to keep cool. The airfield bustled with activity. Three pilots were testing stabilizers on new Aeronca airplanes. They would take off, circle the field twice, and land, almost in formation. It was fun to watch.

In less than half an hour, Nick returned, carrying the part in a paper sack. The two took off, turned northwestward, and leveled out at 3,000 feet. Nick immediately set the stabilizer, stuck a small pillow against the left window, and in moments was sound asleep. Max pulled out a comic book and started reading. Chances of meeting another plane in flight were virtually nil, and with little wind there was no chance the plane would wander off course.

Max was not sure how long he read before glancing out at the ground, but he guessed some fifteen minutes. When he looked down he gasped. There was nothing below but ground fog.

Max hit Nick on the arm and yelled, "Look!" pointing downward. Nick immediately took the wheel and turned the airplane in a circle to the right. As far as they could see, there was nothing but fog.

"We got troubles," Nick called out as he turned the airplane on a northwest course, following his compass. With no radio it was impossible to communicate with anyone. Nothing was sticking up through the fog, so there was no way of knowing exactly where they were.

"I'm going down to see how high the fog extends," Nick yelled, circling counter clockwise rather than diving to the level.

When Nick reached one hundred feet, he leveled out and said, "I'm afraid to go any lower, but we can't be more than twenty or thirty feet above it. Looks like solid ground fog. I only hope it breaks up before we reach Lynn."

The two flew in silence for several minutes before Nick recognized a water tower sticking above the fog at the edge of an Ohio town and turned slightly north. Some fifteen minutes later they spotted the top of the water tower at Lynn and knew they were over the airport.

"I'm going to fly a pattern back and forth from Lynn to Fountain City," said Nick. "Watch for any dark spot in the fog, for that might show us an opening. We've got enough gas for about an hour, and that is it. Look sharp. We need that opening."

The towns lay seven miles apart. Nick could guess where the airport was located, but the water tower was the only thing sticking up through the fog. Only one time did Nick see a dark spot, but it quickly closed.

Neither Nick nor Max talked as they flew the pattern over the airport. Max's eyes watered from straining to see any opening in the fog. But there was none. The fog seemed endless as it covered the ground below, showing a slowly rolling motion that went northeast.

After thirty minutes Nick had Max take the wheel so he could relax his hands a few minutes and contemplate what he might do. Max circled over the Lynn water tower. He knew he was passing directly over the airport, but as far as the eye could see there was nothing but that crawling gray mass.

In the early days of flying there were no radio beams to follow from city to city. Following highways was impossible due to sudden changes in direction. So pilots followed the railroads, studying charts that showed the various rail lines that left or entered a city and mapping their destination from those charts.

Nick and Max flew to the Aeronca factory in Ohio to purchase a part for an Aeronca K airplane, similar to the one shown here. An economical airplane, the Aeronca K was introduced in 1937 and was an immediate hit with private pilots and flying schools across the country.

"We are down to no more than ten minutes of fuel," Nick called out, pointing to the gauge. "Let me take it back. I'm going to sweep back to Fountain City one more time, and if we do not find an opening I will have to guess at the field and hope we get lucky."

Five more minutes went by, and Nick said, "This is it. We've got to get this airplane down now while we still have power."

At that moment Max yelled and pointed, "Nick! Look west! Is that an opening?"

Nick quickly turned toward the dark spot and, sure enough, the fog had parted over an area about the size of a baseball diamond. The opening was moving northeast toward the airport. Nick settled over it in tight circles no more than fifty feet off the ground.

"Young man," said Nick, "pray like you've never prayed before that this opening does not close."

The gas gauge said empty as the two continued to circle. Suddenly Nick yelled, "The tree!" Pilots at the field, while learning to fly, kept their plane straight to take off south as they picked up speed by aiming at a huge tree some half-mile away. There was no doubt. It was the tree.

"The opening is going to miss the runway," Nick called out, "but I'm going to guess on distance and put it down. We're out of gas."

Nick turned the plane north over the tree and reached to pull back the throttle. At that moment the engine sputtered and quit. Out of gas. As Nick headed into a solid bank of fog, the only noise was the wind rushing past the fuselage. It seemed an eternity to both pilots.

Max yelled, "The fence!" as it suddenly appeared with the plane headed straight into it. Nick pulled back on the wheel, and the airplane hopped over the last obstacle, scraping the rear wheel as it settled onto the edge of the airport runway.

The plane rolled to a stop. Neither pilot moved. Then Nick looked at Max, grinned, and said, "A piece of cake!"

At that moment a red Ford pickup truck came skidding to a stop next to the plane. Clarence and Minnie jumped out and ran to the door as Nick pushed it open. They had endured more than an hour of listening as the plane flew back and forth over the airport, knowing the fuel was getting lower and lower.

Max admitted later that never in his many years of flying was he more scared than the moment when the engine died and all he could see was fog.

HANGAR FLYING USA
Lindbergh's Transatlantic Flight

When thinking of close calls in flying involving fog, none matches the performance of Charles Lindbergh, the first person to fly solo nonstop across the Atlantic Ocean. The year was 1927, and the Ryan monoplane Lindbergh had helped to design was dubbed the Spirit of St. Louis.

In 1922 Lindbergh had dropped out of the University of Wisconsin to enroll in a Lincoln, Nebraska, flying school. One year later he purchased a World War I Jenny and began soloing and barnstorming. He later flew cross-country delivering airmail, and when he learned about the $25,000 Orteig Prize for the first person to fly nonstop across the Atlantic, he persuaded a group of St. Louis businessmen to back him in his attempt.

Lindbergh departed Roosevelt Field in New York on May 20, 1927, at 7:52 a.m. He landed at La Bourget Field in Paris, France, on May 21, 1927, at 10:22 p.m. local time. The 3,600 mile flight took thirty-three and one-half hours. The plane was customized so that Lindbergh had extra fuel. The cockpit was moved to the rear due to the added fuel tanks, and the pilot used a periscope to look over the hood of the plane.

Bad weather and the possibility of postponing his transatlantic flight met Lindbergh on his arrival in New York. Although the field was soft and muddy from the rain, he attempted his takeoff after a report of improving weather. After gathering speed slowly and becoming airborne, Lindbergh's plane cleared a telephone line by only twenty feet.

AMELIA EARHART PHOTOGRAPHS AND POSTERS COLLECTION, INDIANA HISTORICAL SOCIETY

No two figures were better known in the early days of flying than Charles Lindbergh and Amelia Earhart.

As with Max and Nick on the flight from central Ohio, fog was the one great danger Lindbergh faced. He encountered fog shortly after he began flying over the ocean. The fog thickened for the next two hours and was troublesome even at 10,000 feet up. Storm clouds above the fog kept Lindbergh from flying any higher. So, he was forced to fly only a few feet above the ocean. Miraculously, as he neared Ireland, he was only a few miles off course. Fortunately, the fog cleared as the weary pilot approached France, and Lindbergh landed under perfect conditions.

CHAPTER NINE

The Parachute Jump

It is vital that you pull the rip cord before you reach the ground.

Clarence, Minnie, and Max were seated at the breakfast nook in their country home next to the airport when there was a knock on the back door. Max hurried to answer it and found a young man standing there with a parachute over his shoulder.

"My name's Chet," he said. "Is your father home?"

Max called to Clarence, and he came to the door.

"I'm a professional parachute jumper, and I've got an idea where we can make some money," the man said to Clarence.

"Well come on in," said Clarence, opening the door. "I'm Clarence Knight, and I'm always in the mood to make a profit. What do you have in mind?"

Chet walked into the kitchen. After being introduced to Minnie and Max, he laid his parachute on a chair and accepted the cup of coffee offered to him.

"I want to jump off the top of the Lynn water tower," said Chet, taking a sip as he talked. "And since you own the airport, I thought you would be a good one for the promotion."

Clarence looked at Chet like he was off his rocker. "That is the dumbest idea I have ever heard," he said. "Your chute wouldn't open before you hit the ground. You would kill yourself."

"No," Chet replied. "The water tower is a little over one hundred feet high. If I tie my rip cord to the upper rail, the chute will start to open as soon as I jump, and it'll open before I hit the ground."

Clarence continued to tell the young man he was out of his mind to try such a thing. Then Chet said, "Clarence, let me prove it to you. If you can find a couple guys willing to climb the tower, I'll have them carry whatever weight they can manage to the top, tie it to the chute, and give it a shove. I'll show you I'm right."

Clarence reluctantly agreed. "But," he said, "I don't want word to spread about this until we're sure it can be done. I am not going to let you kill yourself in front of dozens of people. I know a couple men who will help us. We'll check this out late at night when no one is around."

At midnight three nights later, Clarence, Chet, and Max met Jimmy Houser (Crackshot Houser's son) and Pat Blansett at the base of the water tower. Jimmy and Pat often helped Clarence at the airport, and Pat had visions of becoming a parachutist himself. The two men climbed the tower, each carrying a thirty-pound sack of sand.

When they reached the top, Jimmy hooked the parachute to the weights while Pat tied the rip cord to the tower rail as Chet had told him to do. When all was in place, Jimmy signaled Clarence and Chet by flashlight that they were ready to see what would happen. Clarence gave them the okay with his flashlight, and the men pushed the weights into space. When they hit, the weights buried six inches into the ground.

"See," said Clarence, "I told you it wouldn't work."

"Oh yes it will," Chet answered, jumping around like a dog with an itch. "We only had 60 pounds here. I weigh 156 pounds, more than double. That chute was almost open when the weights hit. It'll open with my weight. No problem." Clarence still thought Chet was crazy to try such a stunt but decided to go along and see what happened.

Word spread like wildfire. Sponsors for the jump kept Minnie busy on the telephone taking down names and the amount they were willing to donate. Clarence had a local print shop run off flyers, and he, Chet, Max, Jimmy, and Pat nailed them to dozens of telephone poles in the Lynn-Fountain City area where they might be read. Virgil Jones, a local man who supplied the loudspeaker system for weekend announcements at the airport, drove through all the surrounding towns, his booming voice over the loudspeaker letting all know of the big occasion.

A Saturday noon date had been set for the daring event. When Clarence totaled up the amount from sponsors, less advertising and other expenses, the two men would be splitting more than $600. In 1938 that was a lot of money.

On Friday evening before the jump, after Minnie had fixed a delicious chicken dinner with all the trimmings, Chet told Clarence he would like to talk to him in private. The two men went into the living room while Max helped his mother carry plates and utensils from the dining room to the kitchen.

COURTESY OF MAX KNIGHT

Chet jumped from the railing atop the Lynn Water Tower. His parachute opened moments before hitting the ground.

Suddenly they heard Clarence shout, "What! I don't believe this. You will jump. I've got to live in this community, while you will be long gone. You are not backing out now." At Clarence's angry insistence, Chet agreed to the jump despite the fear of heights he had just admitted to Clarence.

By noon the next day, the small town of Lynn was overflowing with people. Minnie refused to go, so Max rode in the pickup truck with Clarence driving and Chet hanging out the window on the passenger side. People cheered as the pickup drove through the crowd. Many crowded the truck to touch the daring hero as Clarence came to a stop. Chet climbed out, parachute in hand.

It took several minutes for Chet to reach the base of the water tower as people held out pencils and paper wanting an autograph. Others wanted their pictures taken next to this would-be hero.

Jimmy and Pat were standing at the foot of the water tower as Clarence and Chet approached. Chet handed his parachute to Pat, who slung it over his shoulder and grabbed hold of the tower steps in anticipation of climbing to the top. Chet continued to have his picture taken.

Clarence got Jimmy off to the side and told him what had happened the night before concerning Chet and his fear of heights. "I'll have Pat go first carrying the chute," the airport owner said, "with Chet going next and you bringing up the rear. Be sure you have the chute rip cord tied to that railing so it will open before he hits the ground."

"Don't worry," Jimmy answered.

With the crowd cheering loudly, Pat started up the ladder with the chute over his shoulder. In moments Chet followed him. Jimmy waited until Chet had reached the tenth rung in the ladder, and then he started climbing.

With the crowd continuing to urge him on, Chet reached a fourth of the way; then he stopped, swung one leg around the ladder, reached in his jacket pocket, and pulled out a fifth of whiskey.

Clarence realized what was happening and cried out, "Oh, no! I don't believe this. Not in front of all these people."

A hush fell over the crowd as they watched Chet take a big swig, screw the cap back on, stick the bottle in his pocket, and start once again to climb. When Jimmy saw Chet stop and pull out that whiskey bottle, he looked down for Clarence, wondering if he was supposed to take it away from him. Then he realized it would be impossible, so he continued to climb as Chet climbed. By the time they reached the top, Chet was dead drunk.

Pat held him as steady as possible while Jimmy fitted the parachute to his back. Jimmy had practiced it several times on the ground, so it was no problem hooking it in place. Pat tied the rip cord to the tower railing, and the two men helped Chet move into position. Pat held him on one side, and Chet was leaning against Jimmy's shoulder. The moment had arrived.

"Okay, Chet," Jimmy said as firmly as he could, "you're all hooked up. Jump!" Chet looked down at Jimmy through blurry eyes and said, "Jimmy, I ain't gonna do it. I'll kill myself. I ain't gonna jump. I just ain't gonna do it."

Aerial view of Lynn, Indiana, ca. early 1950s. The water tower appears in the upper right-hand corner. Max Knight took this photo for the Richmond, Indiana, *Palladium-Item* newspaper. Unbeknownst to Max or the newspaper, it was later reproduced as a real photo postcard.

"Look, Chet," Jimmy said, trying to reason with the would-be parachutist, "hundreds of people are down there waiting for their newfound hero to jump. Think how many had their pictures taken with you. Do you want them to remember you as a quitter? You said yourself that with your added weight the chute would open. So, do what you came here to do. Jump!"

Reluctantly, and with a push from Jimmy, Chet went sailing into space, arms flailing, flat on his back as he fell through the air. Thankfully, he had no more than cleared the railing when the rip cord pulled loose and the chute started to open. The terrified parachutist screamed all the way to the ground. The parachute snapped to full width when Chet was about twenty feet from the surface, in plenty of time to break his fall. Chet crawled out from under the billowing parachute and walked away to a tremendous ovation, the hero of the day—and stone cold sober.

HANGAR FLYING USA
Spotters and Paratroopers

Few people used parachutes before the end of the First World War. American pilots generally did not use parachutes during this conflict. However, one branch of the American service was required to wear them. These were the spotters in observation balloons who watched for the arrival of enemy troops. If the balloon was hit by enemy fire, the spotter simply dived into space and parachuted to safety.

During the years between the world wars, barnstormers often performed parachute jumps as entertainment at air shows. At the same time, the military wings of several governments were testing parachutes to determine how they could best be used. During World War II, paratroopers played an important part in the invasion of the European continent. Troops parachuted behind German lines to secure strategic sites such as bridges and roads.

One such paratrooper was Robert Valladon, a Frenchman and Max's close friend who escaped from France, which was held by Germany, to England. Returning as a paratrooper, he worked for several weeks with the French underground in destroying German supply lines and harassing the enemy, helping to open the way for the D-Day invasion.

Paratroopers used a type of packed parachute, which was first popularized in 1890 by the German couple Käthe Paulus and Paul Letteman. The parachutes of the early twentieth century had a canopy apex that was tied to the interior of a canvas bag and to a break cord. The lines and canopy were folded inside the canvas bag with the break cord at the opening. A jumper would clear the airplane, usually by counting to ten, and then pull the break cord, or as it was more commonly called, the rip cord, and the chute would open.

Parachute design has evolved greatly over the years from the round silk parachutes of the 1930s. The parafoil was invented in the 1960s by kite maker Domina Jalbert. The parafoil, also known as the ram-air, has a rectangular shape that allows the jumper to have more control over speed and direction while ascending and landing.

Paratroopers, or soldiers trained in parachuting, were first used extensively in World War II. This photo, taken during the late 1940s or early 1950s by F. K. Ellington of Columbus, Indiana, shows paratroopers in action.

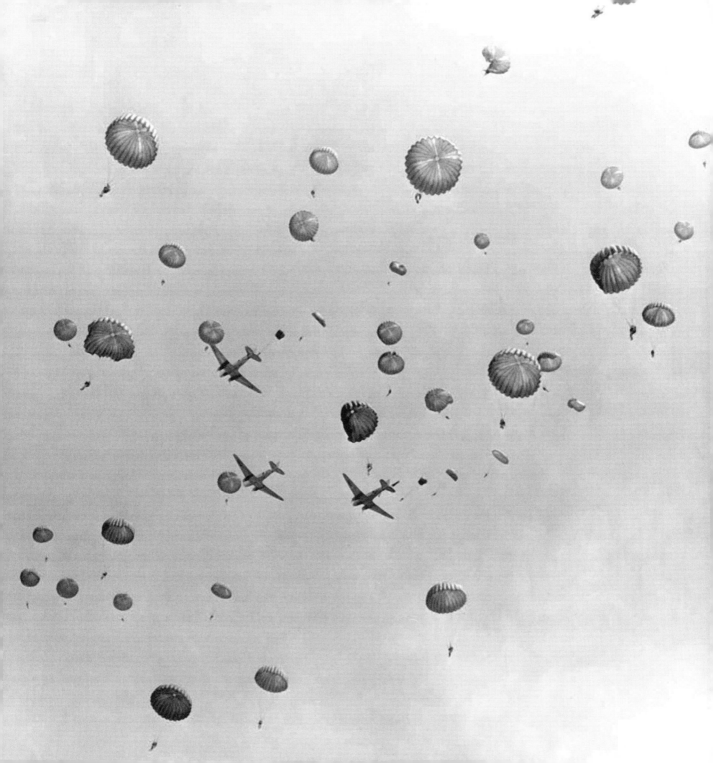

CHAPTER TEN

To Check Out Heaven

*It's better to be down here wishing you were up there
than up there wishing you were down here.*

Uncle Ira Johnson was a Quaker minister. He walked most everywhere he went, including the Knight Airport at Lynn on numerous Saturdays. Seeing Ira walk in was a common sight, and his first stop was always the soft-drink stand run by Max.

"After walking those three miles from home," he always said, "this orange soda renews my energy."

Clarence kept a wooden chair at the north end of the airplane hangar where Ira sat the rest of the day. It was close to the pop stand and in the shade of the building, so he considered it perfect. Max never saw Ira eat throughout the day, but he consumed two or three orange drinks, "renewing his energy."

Ira, in his dark trousers and white shirt, was an unofficial greeter. Many who walked to the hangar stopped to chat with the well-known Quaker minister. He wore a black hat while in the sun but once seated laid it aside. With his hat on, Ira displayed a shock of white hair around the rim, but when he removed the hat, the rest of his head was bald. The fact he sported a short, white beard and full mustache made him a unique figure. Even at his advanced age, Ira still helped pastor two churches, Bethel near Marion and Jericho east of Winchester.

Ira's tremendous smile, which seemed a permanent part of his face, attracted everyone's attention. He had a good word for all who stopped. It was a favorite practice of children to ask him the time of day so that he would pull his big pocket watch out of his vest pocket, flip open the cover, and announce the hour.

Clarence discovered that Ira's ninetieth birthday was in a couple days, so he was waiting by the soft-drink stand one Saturday when the Quaker minister came walking into the airport. It was a bright, sunny day with thin lingering clouds as Ira stopped at the stand for his usual orange drink. At that moment Minnie came walking from the nearby house carrying a huge birthday cake. At least fifty people were there for the occasion. Ira beamed as Clarence led them in singing "Happy Birthday." As Ira blew out the one big candle in the center of the cake, his admirers gave him a rousing round of applause.

It took a lot of persuasion for Minnie to convince Ira the first piece of cake was for him. He wanted to be sure everyone there got a piece. But finally he agreed and appeared to greatly enjoy every morsel.

Clarence, who sang professionally for two years as a young man, told Ira he had a special treat for him. Clarence had learned the Quaker minister's favorite song was "It Is Well with My Soul," so he sang it for all to enjoy. When he finished Ira had tears in his eyes.

With the festivities about to end, Clarence said, "Uncle Ira, you have been here many Saturdays this summer, watching the planes fly and visiting with friends. We greatly enjoy your visits. I am wondering if you would like to take a ride. Nick will fly you over your house and wherever else you want to go, and it won't cost you a penny. How about it?"

The Quaker minister grinned and said, "Clarence, I thought about that all the way out from Lynn. Thee knows I have enjoyed my visits. Yes, I think I would like to go above the clouds and see what it looks like up close. I'm going to be there soon on a permanent basis, and it might be nice to see where I'm headed."

Clarence turned to Nick and said, "Take him low over his house and then top the Taylorcraft out as high as you can get it to go."

"I promise it will be the ride of the century," Nick answered, taking Ira by the arm and helping him crawl into the Taylorcraft seat.

As Nick took off north over the assembled crowd, Ira looked down at a big send-off. People were cheering and waving their hats or handkerchiefs to urge him on. He waved back at them as the plane crossed the end of the runway and headed for Lynn.

Nick flew low around the town, and Ira saw his home quite clearly. He had a big smile on his face as they turned and came back over the house a second time. Then Nick began to climb. He did so by making a large circle from Lynn to Fountain City and at 5,000 feet went through an opening in a thin layer of clouds.

On the ground all eyes were turned skyward watching the plane grow smaller and smaller as it spiraled upward. Soon it was only a dot in the sky, and the people on the ground lost sight of the Taylorcraft as Nick flew above the clouds.

People milled around their cars, still looking skyward when suddenly there was a shout, "Here they come!"

Nick flew low over the crowd with Ira on the side where he could see the people waving, and he again waved back. Then Nick did a wide turn at the south end of the field and headed for the runway.

His landing was picture perfect. As Ira was helped out of the plane, friends and neighbors crowded closer to offer their congratulations. Clarence held up his hand for quiet and then asked, "Well, Uncle Ira, what do you think?"

In that deep Quaker voice many knew so well, Ira said, "Clarence, it's even more beautiful than I thought it would be. Thee hast done me a great service. I am ready to go."

He did—at the age of ninety-three.

HANGAR FLYING USA
The Flying Evangelist

At six o'clock every morning Clarence turned on the radio and listened to a program from Indianapolis known as the Cadle Tabernacle, *officially named* The Nation's Family Prayer Period. *The program started with Ola Cadle playing and singing the song "Did You Think to Pray?" Then her husband, evangelist E. Howard Cadle, offered prayer, and the program was underway.*

Howard regularly drew a crowd of around 4,500 people at the Cadle Tabernacle, located in downtown Indianapolis. The Cadles also traveled frequently to nearby states. Known as the "flying evangelist," Howard and Ola would get in their private airplane virtually every week, and their son Buford would fly them to some city in Kentucky, Tennessee, Ohio, or West Virginia, where they would hold evangelical services.

Clarence was at the Indianapolis Municipal Airport when the Cadles' plane returned from one of its trips, barely avoiding a fatal crash. As the plane was descending, a J-3 Piper Cub rolled onto the apron at the end of the field to take off. While moving forward the pilot suddenly realized there was an inbound aircraft and quickly gunned the engine and swerved to the grassy area beside the runway.

At the controls of the Cadles' plane, Buford landed the plane safely, but hard. Along with several others, Clarence ran to the plane to make sure no one was injured. The J-3 pilot rushed to the Cadle aircraft as well and apologized profusely. Buford rebuffed the apology in a rough manner, however. He was quite upset, for if the pilot had continued with his takeoff, a crash would have been impossible to avoid. Fortunately, the crash did not take place. E. Howard Cadle lived until 1942. Clarence, however, was so upset by the incident that he never listened to the Cadle hour again.

The Reverend E. Howard Cadle broadcast from the Cadle Tabernacle (pictured here), located in Indianapolis, early each morning. He owned his own airplane for evangelic trips to surrounding states. Cadle's son Buford was his pilot.

CHAPTER ELEVEN

Solo Experiences

*You know you've landed with the wheels up
if it takes full power to taxi to the hangar.*

It was not unusual for students to solo after only three or four hours of instruction. There was no set rule on how many hours of instruction a pilot should have, as there is today. It made for some interesting stories.

Bob was a law official who came to the field on business and stayed to learn to fly. But Bob was an erratic pilot, showing excellent ability on one flight and insecurity on another. Nick was concerned.

The instructor had Bob practice takeoffs and landings over and over, far more than the normal amount of time required for him to learn the proper procedure. On one landing Bob would be perfect. The next time around he would be all over the place. Finally Nick decided he might as well turn Bob loose and hope for the best.

"I can't teach him anymore," Nick told Clarence. "Let's take a chance and let him solo."

They picked a day in the middle of the week when few people were at the airport. Nick flew around with Bob one last time, crawled out of the plane, shut the door, and motioned Bob to take it up. Bob, with a serious look on his face, gave Nick a thumbs-up sign.

The student pilot went to the south end of the field, headed north, opened the throttle, and took off like a veteran. Both Nick and Clarence gave a sigh of relief. He was in the air. Now to get him back down in one piece.

Bob circled the airport four or five times and then headed in from the south to land. Nick and Clarence crossed their fingers as Bob cut the throttle to glide in. He was much too high and gunned the motor to go around again.

"That happens often on first solo flights," Nick said, more to himself than to Clarence.

As Bob approached the runway from the south a second time, it appeared he was right on course, but suddenly he gunned the motor, and back up he went.

The two men on the ground sweated profusely as Bob tried three more times to land the plane, and each time he was too high to get it down.

After the fifth try, much to Nick and Clarence's surprise, Bob did not circle for the approach again. Instead he suddenly headed north from the airport and soon was out of sight. Both men were flabbergasted.

"Goodbye airplane," Nick said. "He's gonna crash sure as can be."

"Do you suppose we ought to take the truck and try and follow him?" Clarence asked.

"Not much use," Nick answered. "He's out of sight already. Might as well go over to the house and see if we get a telephone call from someone who sees him go down."

The two worried men hurried to the nearby house, told Minnie what had happened, and waited. No more than ten minutes later the phone rang.

Clarence answered. His conversation went like this, "What? You did what? Why? Are you all right? We'll be right there." As he hung up, Clarence turned to Nick and could hardly talk for laughing.

"What in the world?" Nick asked.

When he could control himself, Clarence answered, "That character decided our field was too small to get into so he flew to Winchester and landed on Everett Cox's longer runway. He wants you to fly the plane back home."

It was the only time in the history of the airport that a pilot, while soloing, landed in the wrong field.

Bob later mastered the smaller field and flew out of it many times. But he never lived down his first solo flight.

At the smaller airports, learning to sideslip an airplane as you came in for a landing was vital. To sideslip a plane, a pilot slid the plane sideways while flying downward through the air. Both Nick and Lee Crossman made this maneuver part of their early instruction with a rookie pilot. In later years stories came back of pilots who were able to land in a tiny field because they had learned how to sideslip a plane at the Knight Airport at Lynn.

Russell had a total of only three hours of instruction when he talked Nick into letting him take the plane up by himself. Nick was leery even though he realized Russell was a quick learner and had been making excellent takeoffs and landings.

"Okay," Nick said to the young student. "You're a natural, but you realize I'm taking a chance with only three hours of dual time. Remember two things. Go far enough south so you can line up on the center of the runway, and if you do not feel comfortable as you approach, go around again."

As Nick crawled out of the Taylorcraft he glanced back, still wondering if he was making a mistake. Russell grinned at him and waved. Nick shut and locked the door.

The student pilot taxied to the south end of the small field, turned into the wind, and lifted the Taylorcraft off without a hitch. He flew eastward from the airport for a couple miles, turned back, and circled the airport twice before heading into the wind for his landing.

Then the thing that instructors fear most happened. Russell was high enough over the runway to land on a cloud, so he gunned the engine and went around a second time. Then a third time. Then a fourth.

On the ground Nick, Clarence, and Max, as well as a half dozen spectators, were watching the flight. Russell simply was not getting any lower on his landing attempts, and they wondered what he would do.

Instead of circling this time, Russell was approaching the field from the north, downwind and dangerous beyond any question.

"No!" yelled Clarence. "He'll kill himself if he tries to land that direction!"

Russell flew directly over the hangar, and as he did he pulled back the throttle, opened the side door and yelled, "How in the world do you land this thing?"

Some four voices in unison yelled back, "Slip, you idiot! Slip!"

Russell headed into the pattern once more, came in too high as before, laid the plane into a perfect slip mode, and touched down like a veteran. He must have learned well, for he later became a commercial pilot.

There were two women pilots at the Lynn Airport, and both soloed at the field. One, Anita, was a natural. The other woman, Elsie, was anything but.

"I can't believe how fast Anita has learned the basics of flying," Nick said to Clarence as they walked from the hangar to the house. "She really is a natural. The strange part is she was not overly anxious to take flying lessons, but her fiancé kept urging her to do so. Now she is glad she did."

The last eighteen months the field was open, Clarence hired a Richmond pilot named Robert (Bob) Moncton to manage the airport. He brought his fiancée, Anita, with him, and both played intricate roles in the continuing success of the field. But Clarence kept his finger in the pie as both a goodwill ambassador and owner.

"Is she ready to solo?" asked Clarence.

"Yeah," Nick answered, "I think she is."

The next afternoon, Bob and Anita drove into the airport wondering if today would be the day Nick would turn her loose to solo. She asked Max if he had a cold Coke, and when he came back with it, Anita and Nick were talking.

"I feel you're ready to solo," said Nick, "but I want you to be ready in your own mind. How about it?"

With a smile Anita answered, "I had a hard time sleeping last night, for all I could think about was being up there alone for the first time. If you think I am ready, then I am ready."

"Okay," said Nick, "let's go around a couple times, and if you still feel you are ready I'll turn you loose to solo."

Her takeoff was perfect. Her flight was perfect. Her landing was perfect. Nick knew she was ready.

"You should be nervous," Clarence said in a kidding manner as Nick crawled out of the Taylorcraft.

"Why?" Anita answered with a smile. "Remember what Nick always says after a total success? Piece of cake!"

She was right. Anita had a flawless takeoff from the runway, circled the airport twice, and on her first attempt made a landing any pilot would have been proud to display for all to watch. When she rolled to a stop at the hangar, she looked over at Nick and, with a laugh, ran her hand across her brow as if to wipe away the sweat.

Anita came often with her fiancé Bob and flew not only the Taylorcraft but also the Fairchild that Clarence considered his more private airplane. Only a select few piloted the Fairchild because it was an underpowered aircraft but a dream to fly.

Max had the privilege of flying with Anita on two occasions, once in the Taylorcraft and once in the Fairchild. He had ridden with so many different pilots by that time he could, in his own mind, tell the good fliers from the mediocre.

After flying with Anita in the Fairchild, he told his dad, "She is one of the very best."

Elsie was a different story.

Elsie purchased an Aeronca K from the Aeronca Corporation at Middletown, Ohio, soon after starting her pilot training. The plane was only two years old, was in perfect condition, and was a high-wing model with strut braces to provide support for the wings.

Elsie, in her midthirties and single, had the Aeronca delivered to the Knight field, and Nick gave her lessons in her own plane. He found she had poor depth-of-field vision, and it worried him enough he told Clarence about the problem. They decided to give her extra hours of dual flying before turning her loose, and it seemed to pay off.

Elsie was given twelve hours of instruction, far more than normal. Finally, the day for her solo flight arrived. Elsie taxied the plane to the north end of the field, turned into the wind, and lifted off without any problems.

She flew for several minutes before turning on her north-to-south route and heading in for a landing. As most often happened on a first try, she was too high. So she hit the throttle and went around again. Twice more she approached the field in direct line with the runway but too high. Nick had given her instruction on how to sideslip the airplane, but she did not try to do so on any of her attempts.

"I was afraid of this one," Nick said to Clarence, rubbing the back of his head. "She's got the ability, but she's afraid of herself."

Elsie flew the Aeronca north from the airport until the men on the ground barely could see it in the distance. Then she circled to her right and once again headed for the field. This time she appeared determined not to be too high as she glided in over the cornfield that bordered the airport on the north.

"Oh no!" yelled Nick. "She's too low. Lift it, Elsie! Lift it!"

"She's going to miss the runway east!" Clarence yelled back. "Go around, Elsie! Go around!"

"She's going too slow!" yelled Nick. By that time Elsie was over the edge of the field, fifty feet east of the runway and low enough her tail wheel caught on a short section of fence Clarence had left in place due to a small swamp area next to the roadway.

The plane seem to be suspended in the air for a moment as the tail wheel hooked the fence; then it simply nosed over into the swamp water with only minor damage. Elsie was not hurt, except for her pride, and later went on to be an excellent pilot.

HANGAR FLYING USA
The Davis Aircraft Corporation

No one preached safety more at the Lynn Airport than Marion (Curly) Kennedy. Curly learned about safety from the *master, Walter C. Davis. Curly worked in the short-lived Davis Aircraft Corporation in Richmond, Indiana, with Davis, a Richmond industrialist who devoted much of his life to aviation. This company built a series of planes that immediately won races in national airshows.*

Davis had served as a pilot and flight instructor during World War I. After his father's automobile manufacturing company was sold in 1928, he acquired the manufacturing rights, parts, and inventory to Vulcan Aircraft's American Moth *plane. Approximately twenty-five airframes were completed at Davis Aircraft between May and December 1929, about half of the planes the company would build in total. Only a few are still flying today.*

Davis's biggest mistake in the building of his aircraft was the date he launched the enterprise. The company's first plane, a two-seater, high-wing monoplane, hit the market only days before the 1929 U.S. stock market crash brought on the beginning of the Great Depression. Overnight, there was virtually no market for Davis Aircraft. In 1932 Davis changed his company into a lawnmower manufacturer, and only a few additional Davis aircraft were built, for racing purposes, from 1933 to 1937. Davis continued flying after his aircraft company failed, and he helped to develop the Richmond Municipal Airport. Walter C. Davis died in 1952.

Davis's employee, Curly, was a native of College Corner and a resident of Fountain City, both in Indiana, and he was the lone mechanic Clarence employed for his airport. He worked a regular job in Fountain City and helped at the airport on evenings and weekends. Safety was a prime factor for the mechanic-pilot, and he pounded it into the heads of those learning to fly. Following are some of Curly's thoughts on aviation safety:

- *Airplanes are safer than cars if you respect them.*
- *There are air traffic rules the same as there are automobile traffic rules. They are to be obeyed.*
- *Your first mistake in an airplane may well be your last.*

Curly's favorite safety observation was this: The flier who demands all a plane can do is a safe pilot. He who demands one iota more is a fool.

This drawing shows a Davis D1 aircraft taking off from the Richmond Airport. The plane performed successfully in local and national aerial events. Marion (Curly) Kennedy, the Lynn Airport mechanic, was always proud that he had helped build the first Davis D1 plane, which was on display in 2007 at the Wayne County Museum in Richmond, Indiana.

CHAPTER TWELVE

A Tanning Machine

It is called a wind sock. If the little end is pointing the direction you are landing, it has been nice knowing you.

On a beautiful June day with the temperature hovering near the 80-degree mark, Martha came driving into the airport late one Saturday afternoon. All eyes followed her as she walked to the soft-drink cooler and asked for a Coke.

Martha was tall and had dark brown hair cropped fairly close. She was wearing a light-colored pantsuit and a smile that was contagious. Clarence, who had been sitting on a bench at the front of the hangar, got up and walked over to where the young woman was standing.

He introduced himself and said, "A young woman like you would not visit an airport to simply watch the planes fly. Are you a pilot?"

Martha smiled and said, "Yes and no. I've been taking lessons up at Kokomo where I've been living, but now I've moved south of Winchester and want to finish up and solo."

She told Clarence her name was Martha and she had logged seven hours of instruction.

"How about going up with our instructor?" Clarence said. "He can determine how much more dual you need to solo. I'm sure you have not flown out of a field this small, so it may be a new experience for you."

Martha readily agreed. Nick took her up and soon realized he had a good student pilot at the wheel of the Taylorcraft. She handled the plane exceptionally well in flight, and Nick had her make a half dozen landings. She was high on her first attempt, but after that, hit the runway dead center with perfect precision.

When they taxied the plane to the hangar and alighted, Nick told Martha to come back as soon as possible as he believed a couple more instructional flights would be enough for her to solo.

A few evenings later, Clarence, Minnie, and Max were seated at the supper table when the telephone rang. It was Martha. She asked if Nick could take her up the next evening, a Thursday. Clarence told her there would be no problem but to come as early as possible.

At four o'clock in the afternoon Martha came driving in and parked her car at the north side of the hangar. She asked Max if he had a bottle of Coke, and in minutes he had run to the nearby house and secured a cold one for her. As she drank the soft drink she talked to Nick and Clarence about flying and how she hoped to use it for an occupation.

"I have no desire to get married anytime in the near future," she told the two men. "I am planning on a future in aviation."

"Maybe," she continued, "it will be in a control tower rather than as a commercial pilot. But first," she laughed, "I guess I better solo and then start planning for the future."

Nick agreed and said he was ready, so the two got in the Taylorcraft. Martha taxied it to the north end of the runway for a takeoff to the south. She shoved the throttle forward and flawlessly lifted the plane off the runway, pulling up to the right as they cleared the end of the field.

Martha made two practice landings, both on the money. After the second touchdown she taxied the Taylorcraft to the hangar area and stopped. Nothing happened for a couple minutes as Clarence and Max watched Nick talking to her. Then the door opened. Nick crawled out of the plane, shut the door, gave Martha a thumbs-up sign, and walked away.

"She's ready," the instructor pilot said to Clarence.

Martha again taxied to the end of the runway and turned the plane into the wind. She opened the throttle and in moments was in the air. The young pilot circled the field twice, flew north over Lynn, and then headed back for her landing. It was picture perfect on her first attempt. Like the good pilots before her, she lightly kissed the ground as she set the Taylorcraft down on the runway. When she taxied to a stop, Max opened the opposite side door on the Taylorcraft and was greeted with a big smile.

Martha flew the Taylorcraft solo five times and then asked Clarence if she could learn to fly the Waco 10 biplane. Nick saw no reason why she should not do so. After four flights with Nick as her instructor, Martha was again ready to solo, and again she had a perfect flight.

For the rest of the summer, every Saturday when the sun was shining, Martha came to the airport, rented the Waco 10, and flew for half an hour. When it was a gloomy, cloudy day, Martha did not show up. No one thought anything about it.

Her pattern was always the same. She flew west for fifteen minutes and then back east for the other fifteen. No one on the ground gave it much thought until. . . .

"You are not going to believe what I just saw!" shouted Frank Baxter to Clarence and Nick as he came running toward the hangar after parking his J-3 Piper Cub.

Frank had flown in from the Nixon Airport at Richmond and had encountered the Waco 10 near Fountain City. He had decided to fly close and wave at the pilot, expecting it to be Martha, for he knew her routine.

"When I flew in over her wing to wave, I realized she was sunbathing while flying!" Frank exclaimed. "She was naked from the waist up, and I darn near hit her plane I was so surprised!"

When Martha landed no one said a word about the incident, but she knew Frank had spilled the beans. As she got in her car, she turned to Clarence and said, "This has been a wonderful experience. There is no way I can thank you and Nick enough for getting me on my way in aviation."

"Hey," said Clarence, reaching over and hugging Martha, "the pleasure has been ours. But you'll be back for more hours in the air, won't you?"

Tears formed in Martha's eyes as she said, "No, Clarence, I'm afraid this is it. I'm moving to Chicago this week and going to work at O'Hare Field [now O'Hare International Airport] in the control tower. I do promise you this. If ever I get close I will stop, but with no family this direction it may be a long time."

Then with a smile she said, "I hope I didn't shake up Frank too much when he zoomed over the Waco. Tell him I said unless he's tried sunbathing while flying, don't knock it."

Not only did Martha work in the control tower, she later earned her rating as a jet pilot and flew delivery for a national company for many years. She never returned for a visit but kept in touch by letter.

When time came to close the airport, Max asked Nick to name the best student he taught during the five years of operation. He did not have to think more than a couple seconds before answering.

"There is no doubt Martha was the best, with Anita close behind. I had some excellent male pilots but none with more natural ability than those two women."

COURTESY OF MAX KNIGHT

Clarence stands beside the Waco 10 that was used to haul passengers at the Lynn Airport.

HANGAR FLYING USA
Women Aviation Firsts

Women have virtually fought their way to the top in aviation since France's Elise Deroche became the first woman to receive a pilot's license in 1910. The next year Hilda Hewlett became the first English woman pilot. She and business partner Gustave Biondeau started a flight school in 1910, and during World War I they opened an aircraft manufacturing facility in Bedfordshire, England. The first American woman to become a pilot was Harriet Quimby, who earned her license in 1911. Quimby soloed across the English Channel in 1912—the first woman to do so.

Another woman to be a first was Bessie Coleman. After American instructors refused to teach her to fly, Coleman traveled to France for lessons, earning a license from the Federation Aeronautique Internationale and becoming the first African American pilot in 1921. Coleman, who dreamed of opening a flight school for blacks, was quoted in the Chicago Defender *stating, "We must have [African American] aviators if we are to keep pace with the times."*

Amelia Earhart is perhaps the most famous female pilot of all time. Among Earhart's achievements was her flight across the Atlantic Ocean in 1932. Earhart was the first female pilot to fly this course. While speaking to a class at Purdue University in 1935, Earhart stated, "Aviation, this young modern giant, exemplifies the possible relationships of women with the creations of science."

First Lady Eleanor Roosevelt wanted to become a pilot and went so far as to receive a student pilot permit during the early 1930s. Although her husband, President Franklin D. Roosevelt, dissuaded her from

Amelia Earhart, 1928. Earhart taught at Purdue University in Lafayette, Indiana, from 1935 until her disappearance in July 1937. Her position was career counselor to women's studies and special adviser in aeronautics. Earhart called the plane that disappeared with her the "flying laboratory."

continuing her plans, Eleanor supported women's ambitions to fly. In 1942, during World War II, she stated, "This is not a time when women should be patient. We are in a war and we need to fight it with all our ability and every weapon possible. Women pilots, in this particular case, are a weapon waiting to be used."

Jacqueline Cochran, director of women pilots for the United States during World War II, held more speed, altitude, and distance records than any pilot in aviation history when she died in 1980. Cochran was in her late fifties when she set her fastest record of 1,429 miles per hour in a Lockheed F-104C Starfighter, a military fighter jet. Commenting later on this flight, she said, "If I had to choose the most exciting adventure I've ever had in the air, I'm sure I couldn't. But flying the Starfighter ranks right up there."

United States Air Force Lieutenant Colonel Eileen Collins is the first woman space shuttle commander. At the official announcement of her position at the White House in 1998, Collins said that she had "dreamed about space" and "admired explorers of all kinds" as a child. Continuing, she said, "It is my hope that all children, boys and girls, will see this mission and be inspired to reach for their dreams because dreams do come true."

CHAPTER THIRTEEN

Curtiss-Wright Pusher

There are old pilots and bold pilots, but no old, bold pilots.
—E. HAMILTON LEE, 1949

A novelty at the Knight Airport at Lynn was Howard Quigley's Curtiss-Wright Pusher. The airplane had an open cockpit at the extreme nose of the aircraft and a second open cockpit midway of the fuselage. The plane's engine sat above the rear cockpit with the propeller on the back side. The propeller *pushed* the aircraft forward—hence the name—instead of the usual pulling motion of an airplane with the propeller at the front.

The Pusher flew at a slower speed than any aircraft at the Lynn Airport. It could stay in the air at a cruising speed of fifty-five miles per hour on a still day. The plane was popular for hauling passengers because, from the front cockpit, a person had a tremendous view of the ground below. Howard had a deal with Clarence to earn fifty cents per passenger, and Clarence furnished the fuel for the flights.

The view from the front seat of the Pusher was beyond description. Max was a frequent passenger in the Pusher, but Howard would not let Max fly the plane because the Pusher did not have dual controls. He said it was too tricky for a child to handle. This was a big disappointment for Max, but it was still a thrill to sit out on the nose of that plane and look straight down.

Clarence, attempting to add variety to the weekend, held a "bombing" contest on Sunday afternoons. All pilots were welcome to try for the grand prize, often ten gallons of gasoline.

For the contest Clarence used powdered lime to draw a circle containing a three-foot-wide bull's-eye in the middle of the field. Pilots flew at different altitudes for different prizes, dropping one-pound sacks of flour at the target. The drop closest to the bull's-eye at the end of the day won the grand prize.

The Pusher was a perfect plane to fly for "bombing" the target. An individual could lean over the front end of the plane, sight the bull's-eye, and fire away. One day Max made the mistake of telling Howard his plane ought to be banned from the contest. Bombers from the Pusher had won the top prize for three straight weeks. Max did not realize it at the moment, but his criticism upset the Pusher owner.

A few minutes later, Max and his helper, Paul Stout, were refilling the soft-drink tank when Paul glanced upward and yelled, "Look out!" At that moment a one-pound sack of flour landed dead center in the tank, covering both boys with water, flour, and ice. They looked up to see Howard dipping the wings of the Pusher in victory.

Back on earth, Howard apologized for making such a mess, and Max apologized for his remark. After the two shook hands, Howard spent the next two hours helping Max and Paul clean out the tank, wipe off all the flour-covered bottles, pour in fresh water and chunks of ice, and get the business open again.

Later that summer, Howard and Bob McDaniels were extremely fortunate when a totally unexpected problem arose as they were barreling down the runway in the Pusher, only moments after lifting off the ground. Bob was flying from the seat at the center of the plane, directly in front of the propeller, and Howard was in the front seat. As the plane lifted off the ground, the propeller shattered, sending pieces of wood flying in all directions. How the flying wood missed Bob was a miracle. But it did, and he was able to get the plane back on the ground without further damage.

Investigation of the accident revealed that one piece of the wooden propeller had gone through the fuselage six inches from the back of Bob's head. Bob, who flew for the airlines for many years, later remarked that the incident with the Pusher was the closest he ever came to being killed in an airplane.

Howard's father, Art Quigley, was sheriff of Wayne County, the county adjoining the Lynn Airport. Art often visited the airport but told his son he never would ride in that death trap called a Pusher. In fact, he often kidded his son about his flying box that did not even look like an airplane.

Howard, however, loved flying his Pusher and repeatedly told his father it was quicker getting places without all that traffic. Both men were standing by Max's soft-drink tank when Art tossed out the ultimate challenge.

"Son," said the sheriff, "I will bet you five dollars I can beat you from here to the Nixon Airport at Richmond. You fly your Pusher, and I'll drive my Packard."

"You're nuts, Dad," Howard answered.

"Five dollars says I'm not," Art replied, pulling his billfold from his pocket.

"Okay," Howard answered. "I'll gladly take your money."

Howard crawled into the Pusher. The propeller was spun and the engine fired. He had to take off south to north, meaning he was headed in the opposite direction from the Richmond Airport on takeoff.

Art tipped his Coke bottle for the last sip and tossed the empty to Max. "See you later," he said to Clarence.

He then settled into his Packard, flipped on the red roof light, and punched the siren. Art and the Packard sped away spraying gravel as they headed out of the airport. The Wayne County Sheriff was standing in front of the hangar at the Richmond Airport drinking a Coke when his son rolled to a stop in the Pusher. Art walked to the plane. Without saying a word, he held out his hand and took the five dollars from Howard. Then Art got in his car and drove away.

Howard Quigley stands in front of the Taylorcraft airplane in the hanger at Knight Airport in Lynn, Indiana, in 1939. Sitting in the middle of the bench in the background is Clarence Knight.

The demise of Howard's Pusher came about in a strange and totally unexpected way. Howard, who kept his Pusher at the Richmond Airport most of the time, did not have a hangar to house the plane in. Instead, when he knew he would not fly for a few days, he anchored it down with cables on each wing and on the tail.

On a very windy mid-April day, Howard flew to Muncie to go through a routine inspection to renew the plane's license. He was hoping the inspector could wrap things up by late morning so that he could head back before conditions got any worse. But as luck would have it, the inspector already had five planes ahead of Howard's. By the time the inspection was over and Howard was ready to head for Richmond, it was midafternoon and even windier than before.

Howard took off without a problem, but all the way home had to battle a crosswind that required him to use every ounce of flying knowledge he possessed to keep the plane on line. With a big sigh of relief he arrived, heading into the southwest runway at the Richmond Airport and landing the Pusher without incident. Howard taxied to the hangar, cut the engine, and hurried to see if someone could help him back his plane to where tie-downs were anchored in the ground. One man was available. As they ran out the front door of the hangar, a huge gust of wind hit the Pusher and flipped it over. In an instant the Pusher was totally destroyed and never flew again.

Al Heath, comanager of the Richmond Airport, lost his plane in the same windstorm. He had flown his Brunner Winkle Bird CK to Muncie for a routine check and landed only moments after Howard landed his Pusher. Seeing the Pusher upside down, Heath tried to get his plane to the side of the hangar away from the wind but did not make it. He was not injured when the wind tipped the plane over, but the plane was badly damaged.

Howard was a daredevil, even on the ground. One time, Clarence had an airplane engine go bad and decided to find a replacement. After searching for a couple weeks he discovered the exact model he needed was at Camden, Ohio. He drove to Camden with Nick, and after checking it over, Clarence made the purchase.

Back at the airport Clarence, who also operated a trucking business, decided he better send one of his trucks to get the big engine. But he hated to pull a truck off its regular run for the biggest part of a day to make the trip. It was then Howard volunteered.

"Let me and Fred Adelsperger go get it," he said to Clarence. Fred was a young man of seventeen from Richmond who had learned to fly and would continue to do so for many years. "I'll take the back seat out of my car, and that opens it to the trunk. I'm sure we can get it in the back without a problem." Clarence debated but finally agreed, and by late afternoon, Howard and Fred headed for the southwestern Ohio town.

The two got to Camden soon after dark and found the engine and the man who sold it to Clarence. He had the engine rigged with a pulley, hanging some five feet in the air. Howard carefully backed his car under the engine but soon realized it would not fit in the trunk without being turned. So Howard pulled the car forward, and the men turned the engine sideways. Howard then backed the car under the engine once again.

They eased the engine down into the car, and, sure enough, it fit with an inch to spare. The engine's weight, however, brought the front end of the car almost off the ground—any little bump in the road and the front end of the car would be airborne.

The men worked for an hour easing the engine forward in the trunk until part of it extended into the backseat. It was eleven o'clock at night when Howard and Fred slowly drove out of the driveway. They crept toward the edge of town at about fifteen miles an hour. Suddenly a red spinning light appeared in their rearview mirror.

"Oh, no, a cop!" Howard said. He pulled over to the side of the road and stopped.

The policeman approached the vehicle with his gun pulled from its holster. He thought the two men had a safe, as from a robbery, in the backseat, and he was not taking any chances. Howard tried to explain what they were transporting, but the officer made them get out of the car, lean against the vehicle, and spread their legs. Howard kept pleading with the officer to look in the trunk, but he was not about to do so until he was sure the two men were not armed.

Finally the officer looked in the trunk of the car. After one look he said, "Even my grandchildren won't believe this."

Howard and Fred arrived back at Lynn, engine intact, at three o'clock in the morning.

HANGAR FLYING USA
Pusher Planes

The Curtiss-Wright Pusher was seldom used for stunt flying due to its cumbersome body and small engine. Howard Quigley's aircraft featured a 39-horsepower Szekely engine, the smallest on any plane kept at the Lynn Airport. The 40-horsepower Taylorcraft, which Clarence purchased in October 1936 after opening the field in August, was also underpowered, but the difference one horsepower made in overall performance was amazing.

Because of its unique look—having a propeller at the back that pushed the plane forward—the Curtiss-Wright Pusher was a novelty and a big hit at air shows in the 1930s. However, landing was an experience. The plane was nose heavy with a passenger in the front cockpit. The pilot had to "mush" the plane onto the runway, meaning he or she pulled back on the stick, causing the plane's nose to lift into the air, landing nose high.

Landing caused many first-time passengers in the front seat to break out in a cold sweat. When the pilot lifted the nose to mush in, the passenger could see only blue sky. The passenger was sure the plane would crack up.

Many of the early airplanes were Pushers. Two of these were the Wright Flyer and the Curtiss Model D. The Wright Flyer became famous when Orville, and then Wilbur Wright, successfully flew it at Kitty Hawk, North Carolina, on December 17, 1903, opening the era of human flight. The Model D gained fame by becoming the first plane to land on a ship. Eugene Ely landed a Curtiss Pusher Model D on the deck of the USS Pennsylvania *on January 8, 1911.*

This photo from the scrapbooks of pilot Eugene B. Ely shows Ely landing a Curtiss Pusher biplane on the USS *Pennsylvania,* which was anchored in San Francisco Bay in 1911.

CHAPTER FOURTEEN

Flying Death Traps

*Always try to keep the number of landings you make
equal to the number of takeoffs you make.*

To call the pilots of those early days of flying "daredevils" would be a perfect description. Anything that had wings and an engine was fair game for flying.

Clarence had seven planes anchored at the Knight Airport at Lynn, but when the opportunity arose to have a Travel Air on display, he could not turn it down. The Travel Air was a big airplane, actually huge compared to the small Taylorcraft Clarence owned.

The plane Clarence saw at the Nixon Airport at Richmond was a two-wing aircraft, painted totally black. It featured a 160-horsepower Curtiss C-6A engine, an engine much larger than any plane held at the Lynn Airport. He knew it would be a conversation piece for visitors, and he would set it up so that people could sit in either of the two big cockpits. Pilot Bob McDaniels at the Richmond Airport said that, during the past year while the plane was open for visitors to examine, he estimated that more than two hundred people had played pilot in its cockpits.

After Clarence worked out a financial deal with Bob, Frank Baxter, a local pilot who often stopped by the Lynn Airport, agreed to deliver the Travel Air to Clarence. The problem was the big plane had not been started for almost a year because it simply had been on display for looks at Richmond.

Clarence had mechanic and pilot Marion (Curly) Kennedy check out the Travel Air engine. After the inspection Curly told Clarence that he doubted the plane would start. The engine was rusted and in terrible shape. Clarence instructed Curly to do what he could, and after three days of work the mechanic gave it a try. To the surprise of all, the huge engine fired on the third attempt. After sputtering for what seemed like several minutes the engine caught and purred away.

Frank taxied the Travel Air around the Nixon field, reaching air speed before backing off and keeping the plane on the ground. For another hour Curly worked on the plane, making adjustments, and finally Frank was ready to fly it to Lynn.

The engine was shut off, and the mechanic gave it a final check while two men filled the gasoline tank. The Travel Air held fifty gallons of fuel, and no leaks were found that would hinder Frank's seventeen-mile trip to the Lynn Airport.

Clarence and Max headed for Lynn in their red pickup truck while the plane was being serviced. Clarence had told Frank not to fire up the plane until they reached the Lynn Airport and phoned to say they were ready for him to make the flight.

This Travel Air plane sat on display at the Knight Airport in Lynn, Indiana.

It took four tries before the engine fired again, and the Travel Air appeared ready for takeoff. Frank let the engine warm up as he taxied to the northeast corner of the Richmond Airport and turned southwest into the wind. When the engine was ready Frank revved it up to make sure it would not fail, eased the throttle back, and glanced at the wind sock. Then he shoved the throttle forward, and the plane started to move.

Frank immediately smelled gasoline but thought little of it, hoping the men had spilled some while filling the tank. But when he lifted off the ground he saw a stream of gas shooting from the left side of the plane past the cowling, a cover housing the engine. He knew it was a dangerous leak. He thought about circling around and landing but decided that since he was already in the air it would be no more dangerous to fly the seventeen miles to Lynn and land than it would be to set the monoplane back down on the airport below him. So Frank very carefully banked the Travel Air to the north and headed for the Lynn Airport.

The gasoline was still shooting out as Frank straightened the plane for level flight, when he suddenly saw a second stream of gasoline shoot from the opposite side of the engine. This presented a problem, for turning the plane either way might cause the gas to spray onto the hot engine and start a fire. All he could do was keep the plane as level as possible and continue to fly northeast toward Lynn.

As Frank approached the town of Fountain City, he had only five miles to go. A quick check of the altimeter told him he was flying at 500 feet. At that moment the engine sputtered and with a loud cough, quit cold—it was out of gas. Fifty gallons had either been spewed out or consumed in less than ten minutes in the air.

Frank quickly looked down and saw the high school baseball diamond directly in front of him at the north edge of the small town. He dropped the nose of the plane, praying he could clear the fence around the field, and headed for the diamond, landing downwind, often a fatal mistake. But he had no choice.

The land rushed up to meet him, but that trusty old Travel Air mushed as Frank pulled up on the nose and touched down like a baby being placed in a crib. The plane rolled to a stop some ten feet from the end of the playing field.

Clarence and Max, in the meantime, were standing outside the Lynn Airport hangar listening and looking for the plane to appear. When it did not, they were sure Frank had crashed. At that moment Minnie came out the back door of the house and yelled that

Frank had landed the plane on the Fountain City ball diamond when the engine quit, and everything was all right.

Clarence finally got the plane to Lynn two days later. A friend used a flatbed truck to haul it the rest of the way after Curly and two other men removed the wings.

Max always bragged that he and Frank Baxter were the only two who got to ride in the Travel Air—and it was true. Clarence allowed his son to sit in the pilot's seat while the men hauled the airplane fuselage from the Fountain City baseball diamond to the Lynn Airport.

Although Frank said that the trip in the Travel Air was the most dangerous flight he ever experienced, had it not been for Max's friend Paul Stout, Frank might have died a horrible death two weeks after flying the Travel Air. Max and Paul were working at the soft-drink cooler, and Frank was looking through a clipboard filled with inspection reports he had to complete before flying to Muncie that afternoon. He had come to the Lynn Airport to talk with Clarence about the reports since the Lynn owner had recently finished his inspection.

Fully concentrating on the reports, Frank walked as he read, and without realizing where he was, headed directly toward the stopped Taylorcraft. Nick was talking to a student in the plane, which was idling with the propeller spinning.

Clarence was the first to see what was happening. He yelled Frank's name and started running from the hangar toward Frank. There was no possible way he could get there in time, and Frank could not hear him above the idling airplane engine.

Max and Paul heard Clarence shout and looked up to see Frank only three or four steps from that spinning propeller. His head was down as he read off the clipboard, and they, too, realized he was slowly walking into the spinning propeller.

Paul, who was a pitcher on the Lynn Junior High School baseball team, reached down, grabbed a rock, and in one motion, threw it at Frank. The rock hit him in the middle of the back. He looked up and swerved to the side, missing the deadly propeller by no more than three feet.

The next time Frank flew up from Richmond on a Sunday afternoon, he presented Paul with a new baseball and fielder's glove. It was the first glove Paul ever owned, and it became a prized possession.

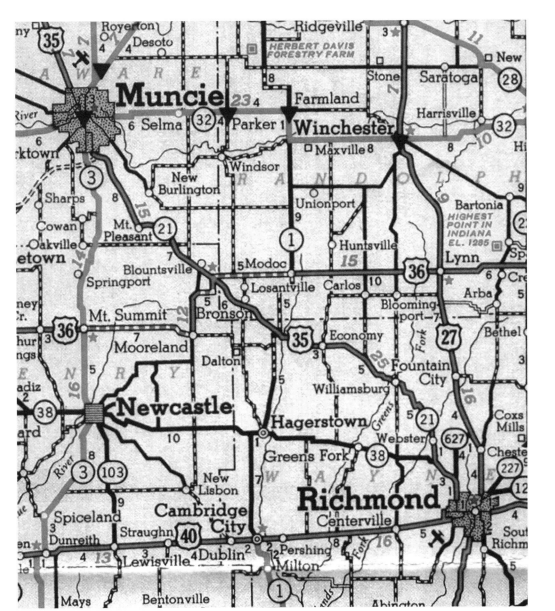

1930s era map of Lynn, Indiana, and surrounding area from "Official Road Map, Indiana" (Chicago: H. M. Gousha Co., 1933-36), Indiana Historical Society

HANGAR FLYING USA
The First Passenger Flights

Ten years after the Wright brothers' first flight at Kitty Hawk, the very first passenger flight took place. On January 1, 1914, Abraham C. Phiel, former mayor of St. Petersburg, Florida, paid $400 for the honor of being the first passenger on a commercial flight. The wooden-hulled "airboat" belonged to the St. Petersburg-Tampa Air Boat Line and raced the twenty-three miles between cities at around one mile per minute.

The airline lasted only four months. It drew business daily, charging five dollars for a one-way ticket. With the end of the tourist season that spring, however, the airline shut down and did not resume business.

Passenger flights floundered until 1927, when Charles Lindbergh put flying on the front page with his solo flight across the Atlantic. Afterward, the airplane came of age, and airlines popped up all across the country.

In July 1929 Transcontinental Air Transport offered a unique package that hauled passengers across the country in forty-eight hours. Most of the trip was accomplished in a luxury airplane, the Ford Tri-Motor, better known as the Tin Goose. However, the trip was split between plane and train transport.

A westbound trip typically began at 6:05 p.m. at New York City's Pennsylvania Station, where passengers boarded a Pullman luxury train car for an overnight ride. The next morning, after arriving in Columbus, Ohio, passengers boarded a seventy-four-foot Tri-Motor, complete with wicker chairs and individual reading lights, for a two-hour flight to the outskirts of Indianapolis. Although the Tin Goose could fly for up to six hours nonstop, it made stops every 250 miles for safety concerns and to provide passenger service between cities. During the next leg of the trip, passengers flew to Kansas City and then on to Oklahoma, where the day's travel ended at about 7 p.m.

The second day of travel was more difficult because they flew over various mountain ranges. For passengers with weak stomachs, a train ride could be arranged for the remainder of the trip. After a stop in New Mexico and two stops in Arizona, the Tri-Motor finally made its way toward Los Angeles around 4 p.m. The trip, covering 1,000 rail miles and 2,000 sky miles, took forty-eight hours, twenty-four hours less than covering the 3,000 miles by train alone.

Nevertheless, the business venture failed. One of Transcontinental's planes crashed on September 4, 1929, killing all eight people aboard. When the stock market crashed nearly two months later, passengers could no longer be found who would brave the danger of traveling by air for the extravagant ticket price of $351.94 each way.

This commercial biplane was the standard in flying business class in 1931. The pilot sat in the rear cockpit with the passenger up front. There was a bin set in the side of the plane for luggage.

CHAPTER FIFTEEN

The Tin Goose

*In the battle between aluminum objects going one hundred miles per hour
and the ground going zero miles per hour, the ground has yet to lose.*

Flying in the world-famous Ford Tri-Motor 4-AT was one of Clarence and Max's greatest highlights in flying. Better known as the Tin Goose, the Ford Tri-Motor was the largest civil airplane in the United States when it started passenger service in 1926, the year Max was born. An overnight success, the Tin Goose carried the well-known Ford name and was the first plane to be constructed entirely of metal. Its safety features, including three engines, was impressive.

Bob McDaniels worked for months before finally getting a Ford Tri-Motor at the Nixon Airport at Richmond for a weekend of hauling passengers. Clarence and Max were in the first load of eleven people to make the flight. Normally there were twelve seats, but one had been removed for ease of entry. Neither Clarence nor Max ever forgot the experience.

It was a beautiful July Saturday with the temperature a hot 85 degrees as they walked out to the Tin Goose. Even with all the heat, Max felt a chill go down his spine as he and Clarence readied to board the plane.

Max stood at the foot of the steps looking up at one huge engine at the front of the aircraft and one on each side. The wing above and to his left gave the bulky monoplane the look of a black monster, and Max wondered how something that large could possibly get off the ground.

Clarence and Max entered the cabin and were seated two rows back, Clarence on one side and Max across the aisle. To their surprise the window by their seats had curtains that needed to be pushed back to look outside. An even bigger surprise was to find that the seats were soft wicker chairs instead of cushion-type solid seats. Above his head Max saw that each passenger had his own individual light, used for reading on longer flights.

When those three uncowled 300-horsepower Wright J-6 engines fired up, the noise inside the plane was deafening, and the fuselage vibrated much more than Max had expected. Clarence and Max both put their hands over their ears until the plane started to taxi and the noise and vibration eased somewhat.

Max looked out the side window and marveled at how much higher off the ground they were compared to taxiing in the Taylorcraft. He glanced at the information sheet he had been given and realized it was more than thirteen feet from the ground to the bottom of the wing. The Taylorcraft was not quite six feet tall—a big difference. The huge wing to

Max's left was nearly forty feet long, and from his seat in the plane it appeared to go on forever.

The pilot reached the end of the field and turned southwest into the wind. He sat still for a couple minutes and then suddenly increased the power as he held the brakes to keep the plane from moving. Then with a jolt he shoved the throttle full forward, and the plane started to move. Once again the noise was horrendous, and Max and Clarence again covered their ears. Max expected the plane to take most of the runway to get off the ground and was surprised when the plane moved no more than 300 feet and lifted into the air.

As soon as they cleared the end of the field and the air started rushing past the huge plane, the noise again eased. Still, Max had never been in an airplane where even if you yelled you could not be heard. So instead of talking, Clarence and Max simply looked at each other with big smiles on their faces.

The Tri-Motor turned after only minutes, and in the distance Max could see the city of Connersville. He realized that due to the plane's size it took a relatively wide radius for the plane to complete a turn, so they must have covered half of the twenty-five miles between the two cities before heading north.

Clarence was seated where he could see the two pilots through the open doorway to his front left. Max could see the copilot on the right and part of the instrument panel. They were both amazed at the number of dials and switches on the panel and realized that the copilot on the right was flipping switches and rotating dials while the pilot on the left flew the plane. The copilot must have flipped or rotated a half dozen different mechanisms before they started flying and another half dozen as they were landing. Clarence and Max watched the pilots as much as they looked out the windows.

On his northerly course the pilot passed over Hagerstown before heading back east for his approach to the airport. They were in the air about twenty minutes, but for Clarence and Max it was the experience of a lifetime.

Then they received another surprise. When they passed over the power lines at the north end of the Richmond Airport, they were moving at a higher rate of speed than in the Waco or Taylorcraft. They later learned that the Tin Goose landed at 50 to 60 miles per hour, whereas the Taylorcraft dropped off to less than 50 miles per hour on approach. Stall speed for the Tri-Motor was 58 to 64 miles per hour.

The Tin Goose was kept at the Richmond Airport for two weeks. Bob estimated that more than three hundred people paid their money to ride the huge plane, and there was still a waiting list to ride when the owner of the Ford Tri-Motor fulfilled his contract with Bob and moved on to another airport.

Before Ford Tri-Motor planes made the skies safe for air travel, they were used to deliver mail. They were a tremendous improvement over the smaller, less durable planes that pilots had been flying to deliver the mail to cities large and small. Delivery by the daredevil pilots of these early planes had replaced the railway mail service instituted in 1832.

The beginning of the airmail service was commemorated when Randolph County held a reenactment in the spring of 1938. Clarence took part in the event.

The plans called for all county post offices to take their mail to the central office in Winchester and from there to the Cox Airport at Winchester. Pilot Everett (Coxey) Cox then had it loaded into his Taylorcraft so he could deliver it to Indianapolis. All mail was brought from the outlying towns by automobile, except for Lynn. The Lynn postmaster delivered the mail to the Knight Airport at Lynn, where Clarence, Max, and Nick loaded it into their Taylorcraft, and Nick flew it to the Winchester Airport.

The Winchester Airport was jammed as Coxey roared down the runway, circled east back over the huge crowd, dipped his wings in salute, and headed southwest. Less than an hour later he flew his pattern over the Indianapolis Municipal Airport, got his signal from the ground to land, and delivered the mail as it had been done by bush pilots for many years.

HANGAR FLYING USA
Airmail Service

The initial airmail service pilots are the unsung heroes of early aviation. In their flimsy Curtiss Jennys, de Havilland DH-4s, and other planes of frail design, they fought weather and fatigue to pioneer round-the-clock mail service.

In 1918 the U.S. Postal Service and the U.S. Army joined forces to create the first airmail service. Charles Lindbergh hooked up with two fellow World War I veterans, Bob and Frank Robertson, and flew mail in a de Havilland DH-4 on the St. Louis–Chicago route. Twice during his years of service, Lindbergh had to bail out of his aircraft. After his world-famous overseas solo flight, in March 1929 Lindbergh set up a passenger route for Transcontinental Air Transport and flew the initial run from Brownsville, Texas, to Mexico City, Mexico, in a Ford Tri-Motor. Lindbergh took several sacks of mail with him on that inaugural flight. Oddly, some of the sacks were missing upon his arrival in Mexico. Although the mail sacks were found a month later, the flight is still known as the Lost Mail Flight.

The first U.S. airmail service was a success. So in 1925 the U.S. government invited bids from private contractors to take over the service. Automobile manufacturer Henry Ford was among the first bidders to be awarded a contract for airmail service. He won the right to haul mail along with spare parts he was shipping to his automobile assembly plants in the upper Midwest.

Ford wanted a passenger plane that would give comfortable service to those who rode in it. He purchased the Stout Metal Airplane Company in 1925, adapted plans for one of its existing planes, and was producing the Ford Tri-Motor 4-AT by 1926 to use as a passenger plane and to carry mail.

Although the noise of the Tin Goose was devastating, the plane was a success. With subsequent design adaptations, the three engines and all-metal fabrication made it possible for the plane to fly up to 130 miles per hour while hauling eight to seventeen passengers, two pilots, and an attendant. The main compartment of the Ford Tri-Motor allowed room for a flight attendant to walk through the cabin, serving meals and assisting passengers. Many of the early flight attendants were nurses, as airsickness was a major problem in early flights.

Max took this photo of the Ford Tri-Motor, better known as the "Tin Goose," before boarding the plane for a flight from the Nixon Airport in Richmond. Note the designation "TAT" on the side of the plane. This indicates that it was used by Transcontinental Air Transport, the company that first offered split rail-and-air trips coast to coast.

CHAPTER SIXTEEN

Surprise! Surprise!

Remember, gravity is not just a good idea.
It's the law, and it is not subject to repeal.

Twice during his teenage years of flying, Max encountered the unexpected and lived to tell about it. A third unexpected event—although not life threatening—ended in a flight unlike any he would ever take again.

The first event came soon after Clarence purchased a new Taylorcraft airplane at Alliance, Ohio. The dealer at Winchester, Indiana, Everett (Coxey) Cox, offered to fly it from the factory to the Knight Airport at Lynn. Coxey asked Max if he wanted to come along, and Max readily agreed.

At four o'clock the next morning, Clarence loaded Coxey and Max into his red Ford pickup truck and headed east. Max, sitting in the middle, had brought a pillow, so he laid his head back and slept until his dad stopped for a bite to eat. At noon they rolled into the vehicle parking lot of the Taylorcraft plant.

While Clarence and Coxey went to fill out the necessary papers for the owner transfer, Max walked to the aircraft parking lot to look at the plane. It was beautiful. The 65-horsepower Taylorcraft was blue with red markings, and Max fell in love with it at first sight. He walked slowly around the plane, touching it lovingly like a mother stroking her newborn child. As he turned at the front of the Taylorcraft, Max saw Clarence and Coxey walking toward him. Clarence carried a folder and wore a big smile on his face as he looked at his newest purchase.

Coxey checked out the new airplane from front to back and made sure the gas tank was full. He then turned to Max and told him to crawl aboard.

"See you back at Lynn!" Max called to his father as he opened the right-hand door of the plane. That statement almost did not come true.

Max was in the air virtually every day of the year when the weather was nice. Flying to him was the same as riding in an automobile. He thought nothing of it. Yet, as the plane lifted into the air Max watched the scenery to his right and was rewarded with a view of a beautiful lake. But soon the flight became boring, and the teenager's thoughts went elsewhere. So Max reached into a paper sack he was carrying and pulled out a comic book to read.

As Coxey flew the plane southwest toward Indiana, Max occasionally glanced at the ground and marveled at the sights. It was a beautiful, sunny day, and the temperature hovered around the 80-degree mark.

After flying for almost an hour, Coxey poked Max on the arm and pointed to his left. The Ohio capital city of Columbus was in view. Max watched the skyline for a few minutes and then returned to his reading.

They were flying at an altitude of 4,000 feet and could see far into the distance. With virtually no wind, the ride was as smooth as a freshly ironed white shirt on Sunday morning.

Suddenly Coxey said, "This plane's got a 65-horsepower Franklin engine, and the one your dad traded in was only 50-horsepower. I wonder if it will loop without diving."

Coxey shoved the lever to full throttle and, when the speed increased, pulled the wheel back to loop the plane. There was a problem. Max, with comic books in his lap, had not fastened his seat belt. He was frantically trying to get it hooked as the plane reached the top of the loop. It was impossible. Had the Taylorcraft stalled at the center of the loop instead of going on around, Max would have fallen through the top of the aircraft roof.

But the plane was up to its test, and Coxey completed the loop. Max had started picking up the fallen comic books when Coxey reached over and grabbed his shoulder.

"Young man," he shouted, "don't you ever let me catch you even sitting in an airplane with the engine *off* unless you have your seat belt fastened! You could have been killed back there! That is the dumbest thing I have ever seen in all my days of flying."

Max, his face flushed red, took the scolding without saying a word. When silence returned, Max realized he was shaking from head to foot, and tears were filling his eyes. It was a close call.

Max never again failed to hook his seat belt as soon as he settled into the cockpit. And Coxey never told Clarence about the incident.

The second surprise came on a hot July day with the temperature bouncing off the 90-degree mark and no wind. Max was flying with friend George Polley, and they had taken off from the Cox Airport at Winchester. Max had brought his camera along, and while George flew the plane, Max shot a roll of film. The Randolph County 4-H fair was underway so, as George circled the grounds, Max shot a few pictures. Then they flew down to the Lynn Airport, where Max again took pictures and ended the film shooting session over George's home near Lynn.

"Want to fly awhile?" George asked, and Max, of course, answered, "Sure."

It was such a beautiful day that Max headed for Richmond. The east fork of the White-water River was glistening in the brilliant sunshine as the plane approached the city. It was always a thrill to see the perfect cross the First Friends Church formed as it appeared among the heavy tree foliage at the eastern side of Richmond. It was a beautiful, relaxing flight.

As the plane approached the Winchester Airport to land, George told Max to take it in. Max turned the plane into the wind. The sunshine glistening off the asphalt runway gave the appearance of water puddles, and Max immediately thought of stories he had read about mirages showing up in the heat of a desert. The approach to the runway was perfect, and the plane was settling in halfway down the runway when suddenly it stopped dropping and hung in the air.

"Air bubble," yelled George. "Hang on! I can't help you!"

An air bubble had formed on the steaming asphalt and was holding the plane off the surface. Max had never encountered one before but had heard other pilots tell their experiences. He knew he had to keep the plane as level as possible and pray the bubble broke before they ran out of runway.

The plane rode that air bubble past the airport hangar. The end of the runway was getting closer and closer, and it looked like there was no way to avoid a crash. Max fought the wheel and struggled to keep the plane level.

Suddenly the bubble broke. Max pulled back on the wheel, and the plane hit the runway with a thud that shook them both. The end of the runway was only a few feet away as Max hit the brakes, and the plane skidded to a stop.

George grinned at Max and said, "Good job." Max realized his hands were aching from gripping the wheel so tightly.

When Max and George got out of the airplane to make sure everything was all right, they saw that the propeller was less than three feet from the fence at the end of the runway, and the wheels were only inches from the asphalt drop-off. By this time Coxey, owner of the Winchester Airport, had arrived on the scene.

"I don't know which one of you was flying," he said, walking to the front of the plane, "but I'll tell you this. You did one hell of a job."

That compliment made up for the chewing out Max got from Coxey earlier for his dumb mistake of not fastening his seat belt.

The third unexpected incident that Max experienced in his flying days was one few pilots have ever accomplished. It happened on a windy day when Lee Crossman and Max were flying the 40-horsepower Taylorcraft.

It was a lazy day and the two were flying with no destination. Lee just wanted to fly, and Max went along. As they headed north of Lynn, Lee climbed to 7,000 feet. He asked Max if he wanted to fly awhile, and the teenager took over. Max knew there was a strong wind, but he did not comprehend how strong until taking the controls.

"Boy, that wind is whistling," Max yelled to Lee.

"Might be as much as 30 miles per hour," Lee answered.

The wind was directly from the north, but it was not buffeting the plane as usually happens in a strong breeze. Since it was March, Max was not surprised by the wind, only the density of it.

"I feel like I could stand still," Max said to Lee as he tried to keep the plane level.

"Do you want to have some fun?" Lee asked, grinning at Max.

"Sure," Max answered. "What do you have in mind?"

"Well," said the veteran pilot, "you work the wheel and the rudder bars, and I'll work the throttle. Pull the plane into a stall, and with this wind I think you can hold it there. If so, we can go backward."

Max looked at Lee like he was crazy but soon realized Lee was serious.

"Okay," Max answered, "I'm ready."

Max got the plane in a stall as Lee eased back on the throttle, but Max lost the stall, and the plane went down and to the right.

"Sorry!" Max yelled. "It got away from me. Let's try it again."

In fact, Lee and Max tried it four more times before getting the feel of the plane's motion. For the next ten minutes or so, Max fought the wheel and rudder bars, and Lee worked the throttle. At the end of that time Max yelled, "I can't hold it any longer," and he let the plane drop off again to the right.

"Wow," yelled Max, "that was something! We actually went backward!"

"Yeah," said Lee. "We were just south of Winchester when we got it right. Look down."

Max looked out to the side and recognized the town of Carlos, four miles west of Lynn.

"I don't believe this," Max said with a big grin. "We're at least five miles south of where we started. My goodness, we actually went backward all that distance. If I hadn't actually been in the plane, I never would have believed it happened."

Lee answered with a laugh. "Wait until we try and tell someone what we did. I guarantee we will be deemed a couple of liars."

Liars? Believe what you will. But it really happened.

HANGAR FLYING USA
Hoosier Aviation Firsts

Having a first tied to your name brought fame and fortune to pilots during the Golden Age of Aviation.

Raymond Kelly, a native of Lawrenceburg, Indiana, was an airline pioneer. Born in 1901, he dedicated his life's work to aviation after flying with a barnstormer through Indiana wheat fields. Kelly suffered from an eye condition that restricted his ability as a pilot, so he devoted his talents to designing and manufacturing airplanes. After receiving a degree in mechanical engineering from Purdue University, he helped the United States Army design planes from 1925 to 1928. Kelly met many famous aviators in the early years of flight, including Orville Wright and Jimmy Doolittle. During the Great Depression, he developed new technologies to help pilots fly. One of Kelly's contributions was the altimeter, the instrument that determines the elevation of an aircraft by using measurements of air pressure. Kelly's work also helped prove that passenger jets could outperform the era's "propliners" (large airplanes driven by piston-powered propellers) and smaller jets. Kelly died in 2003 at the age of 102.

The first Hoosier to fly active duty in World War II was Herold Marting from Indianapolis. Marting was a member of the American Eagle Squadron, flying under British authority prior to the United States entering the war.

The first major airfield in Indiana was the Indianapolis Municipal Airport, which opened in 1931 at a cost of $724,000. Soon after its opening a terminal was constructed at an additional cost of $125,000. It was renamed Weir-Cook Field in 1944, a year after Lieutenant Colonel Harvey Weir Cook, Indiana's first World War I ace, was killed in the South Pacific while on duty as a pilot during World War II.

Soon after World War II larger commercial airplanes such as this Trans World Airlines twin-engine airplane were stationed at the Indianapolis Municipal Airport.

CHAPTER SEVENTEEN

Spinning Through Clouds

If all you can see ahead is ground that is going round and round, things are not at all as they should be.

By the time Max was twelve years old, he could spin an airplane with the best of them. Most times spinning, or sending an airplane into a descending spiral with its nose pointed downward, was done simply for fun. But there were other times when it was a safe way to get through the clouds and see where you were going.

Max learned the hard way. One day as he was flying with Lee Crossman, they decided to climb above the clouds. Max started circling slowly as he gained altitude and aimed for a hole in the clouds that proved to be at 5,400 feet.

Through the hole and on top of the clouds there was a beautiful sight. To the west the clouds looked like billowing mountains, daring anyone to fly into them. Below, the smoothness of the white cover gave the false impression that you could land on the clouds without a problem. Both Max and Lee were fascinated with the view.

They flew southeast from the airport as the billowing clouds swirled only yards from the wheels of their Taylorcraft. Often the clouds would suddenly swirl up, and the plane would quickly go through the thin layer.

Since this was the first time Max had encountered such a ride, Lee decided to teach him a lesson.

"I want you to ease down through that cloud ahead and let's go back below them again," said the veteran pilot.

"Do I go straight into them?" asked Max.

"Your choice," came back the answer. "You can slowly dive into them or circle, whichever you want to try."

Max decided to slowly dive, thinking it would get him through the clouds more quickly. He pushed the wheel forward, and in moments the plane was in the total darkness of the cloud. Max quickly became disoriented. Although trying his best to keep the plane going straight, Max suddenly realized the engine was groaning for power, and dirt was falling in his face. He was upside down.

For a twelve-year-old, it proved too much. He panicked, jerked his hand off the wheel, and yelled for help.

Lee took the wheel and pushed it forward and to the right. In moments the plane emerged below the clouds.

"Never," Lee said to a shaken Max, "never try to slowly go down through clouds. There is no way to tell whether you are upside down or left side out unless, of course, you feel dirt from the floor hitting your head, and you suddenly realize you are upside down. Scary, isn't it?"

Max, still frightened, said, "Lee, I've been flying for almost three years, and I've never been that scared before. I had no idea what to do except shut my eyes, let go of the wheel, and hope you could get us down."

Lee started climbing again. Again he went through an open hole in the clouds and leveled out at 6,000 feet.

"Take the controls," Lee told Max. He did so rather reluctantly.

"Now," said the veteran pilot, "lay the plane over in a spin and stay with it until you break out on the bottom."

Max pulled the nose of the Taylorcraft up, kicked the right rudder, and turned the wheel, causing the plane to start spinning to the right. After one full turn and part of a second one, the plane went into the clouds. It continued to spin until it suddenly broke out into clear air, and Max leveled the plane to head back to the airport.

"That is the way you get through clouds," Lee told Max. "Never try it any other way. But, remember, you must be high enough that when the plane breaks through you have plenty of room to flatten out and fly level. That ground down there is mighty hard if you spin into it."

A couple of months later, Max was flying with Bud Knight, his cousin from Danville, Illinois, and he said, "Let's go above the clouds. I want you to try something."

A few minutes later those on the ground saw a blue and red Taylorcraft come spinning out of the clouds directly over the airport. Max was now the teacher.

Taylorcrafts were made to spin. Pusher-type planes were not.

Nick often put on a show for people who came to the airport on weekends to watch the planes. He would do a couple loops and then climb to 7,000 feet before laying the Taylorcraft over in a spin, often rotating five or six times before pulling it out. The crowd would give him a cheer as he alighted from the plane.

Myron (Nick) Nicholson was the primary pilot for the Lynn Airport, taking passengers for rides and teaching students to fly.

Howard Quigley, on the other hand, was often teased about his Curtiss-Wright Pusher flying from the wrong end (the propeller was back of the rear seat and faced backward, "pushing" the plane from the rear). He resented this kidding, and his temper often flared as the ribbing took place. On one occasion, Howard's desire to prove everyone wrong about his plane almost resulted in his death.

Nick landed after one of his aerial exhibitions and said, "Your turn," in a kidding way to Howard.

"Yeah," answered the Pusher pilot, "you just watch."

Howard marched out to the Pusher, had the propeller spun and the engine fired, and took off.

"I don't like this," Clarence said to Max. "He's upset. With his temper I hope he doesn't do anything foolish."

Howard started climbing as he headed south from the airport. When he came back over the runway he was at 5,000 feet. Suddenly his nose went down, and the plane picked up speed. Then Howard pulled the stick back into his lap, and the Pusher did a rather sloppy but successful loop. On the ground the people watching gave him a cheer he could not hear.

"That's enough," Clarence said to no one in particular. "You proved your point. Get back down here."

But Howard was not satisfied. He again climbed to 5,000 feet, and the airmen on the ground knew he was going to try to spin a plane that was not made to spin.

"Don't do it," Clarence pleaded, looking skyward.

Howard pulled the Pusher into a stall, dropped the nose, and shoved the stick right, but instead of spinning the plane flattened out. He tried it two more times, each time getting lower and lower to the ground.

"He's so intent on what he's doing," said Nick, "he's not watching his altitude. If he gets in a spin at that level he won't have time to pull out."

But Howard tried it once more. This time the Pusher, now under 2,000 feet, went nose down, and as it picked up speed, it came closer and closer to the ground. Suddenly realizing his danger, the pilot pulled the stick into his lap and hung tight. The Pusher slowly lifted, missing the top of the hangar by less than fifty feet.

Howard never tried spinning his Pusher again.

HANGAR FLYING USA
Wiley Post

After losing his first plane to fire in 1925, shaking hands with the great pilot Wiley Post at Indianapolis in 1935 keyed Clarence's desire to try flying once again. When Post and entertainer Will Rogers died in a plane crash on August 15, 1935, Clarence broke down in tears.

Post, like Clarence, was a native of Texas. He worked in the oil fields as a young man, and an accident on the job caused him to lose his left eye. With the money from the workers' compensation settlement, Post bought his first airplane, a Curtiss Canuck. He quickly established himself as a professional pilot, but it took winning the 1930 Men's Air Derby Race from Los Angeles to Chicago for him to be noticed in aviation circles.

On July 15, 1933, Wiley became the first pilot to fly solo around the world. It took seven days, eighteen hours, and forty-nine minutes.

1934 found Post working on flying higher, faster, and longer between stops. Backed by the B. F. Goodrich Company, he created an early pressure suit. In official records, Post flew 40,000 feet, and unofficially he flew up to 50,000 feet. Flying this high, Post discovered the jet stream, a long current of high speed winds in the earth's stratosphere, which begins seven to ten miles from the earth's surface.

Always searching for a new challenge, in July 1935 Post decided to survey a mail and passenger air route from the West Coast to Russia but needed a special plane to make the flight. Winnie Mae, *the plane he had made famous in his solo flight, was shelved. Instead, Post flew a hybrid low-wing monoplane with a 550-horsepower Wasp engine, built from a Lockheed Orion and a Lockheed Explorer. The monoplane also featured two gas tanks holding a total of 260 gallons and long floats to use as pontoons.*

Entertainer and close friend Will Rogers accompanied Post. Their itinerary took them from Seattle, Washington, to Fairbanks, Alaska, with several stops in between. After leaving Fairbanks, the plane crashed in a lake about fifteen miles from Point Barrow, Alaska. Sadly, both men were killed.

Will Rogers was honored for his contributions to early aviation by being enshrined in the National Aviation Hall of Fame at Dayton, Ohio, in 1977. Wiley Post received the same honor nearly a decade before, being enshrined in 1969.

Wiley Post (center, wearing eye patch) standing with a group of men in front of his famous plane, the *Winnie Mae*, at Terre Haute, Indiana, in March 1935.

CHAPTER EIGHTEEN

P-51 Pilot Lands Safely

The propeller is a big fan that keeps the pilot cool.
When it stops spinning, the pilot starts sweating.

On a cool June evening in 1940, Jerry drove into the Knight Airport at Lynn and told Clarence he wanted to learn how to fly. Nick had gone to the nearby house for a bite to eat, so Max was sent to inform him he had a student.

Jerry was surprised to learn that Max had been flying a plane since the age of ten, and that made him even more determined to earn his hours and solo. There was a problem, however. Jerry had no money. He told Clarence he would work it out if there was something for him to do, so the airport owner set up a schedule.

Jerry, who lived on a farm near Richmond, came to the airport at four o'clock every Friday afternoon and did whatever chores Clarence had lined up for him to do. He joined Max in wiping down and polishing the Taylorcraft. He helped Max get the ice tank ready for a busy day on Saturday. He spent two evenings nailing down the metal hangar roof that had been pulled loose by March winds. The young man became the jack-of-all-trades at the airport.

Each Friday, before Jerry began his work, Nick took him up for a flying lesson. After the fourth lesson Nick told Clarence that Jerry was a natural. He would make a good pilot. Sure enough, in early September, Jerry soloed, touching down to a perfect landing, something few did on their first solo attempt.

Jerry quickly added up the flying hours as Clarence continued to find work for him to do. By spring he had logged enough hours to get his private license. Max went with him to Muncie, where he passed inspection, and the license was issued. Max flew with Jerry whenever possible, for the young man made flying fun. He was a perfectionist at spinning the Taylorcraft and, although enjoying aerobatics, knew the limits of the airplane and never pushed it to perform.

The first week of June 1941, Jerry came driving into the airport in a swirl of dust, blowing his horn as he stopped. He jumped out of the car waving a piece of paper over his head and shouting to Clarence, "I got it! I got it!"

"You got what?" Clarence asked.

"I got my papers to enter the Army Air Corps. I'm going to be a pilot. I report to the Army Air Corps base at Kessler Field in Mississippi next Friday."

Jerry was so excited he had to tell everyone. He ran to the house to tell Max and Minnie and then got on the telephone to let all the neighbors on the party line know.

Jerry did fly for the Army Air Corps. In fact, he was assigned a P-51 fighter plane after transferring to Texas and, after the war started, went overseas as a combat pilot. He was stationed north of London, England, and had the job of escorting bombers on runs into the heartland of Europe. The fighters could follow the bombers only so far and then had to return to the base due to lack of fuel for a longer range. Every trip out meant a dogfight with German fighters, and Jerry soon had seven kills to his name.

On one occasion Jerry and two other P-51 pilots were nearing the English Channel on their return to England when five German Messerschmitt Bf 109 fighters came out of the clouds to challenge them. Due to their shortage of fuel, they knew they must run for it rather than enter into combat. But Jerry didn't make it. A German pilot got on his tail, and bullets ripped through the left wing and into the engine of the P-51. It stopped cold.

The German pilot had pulled up and was engaging another plane, believing Jerry was on his way to certain death. It was then, as Jerry said later, he thought of the Lynn Airport and how many times he had sideslipped a Taylorcraft to get it into the tiny twenty-acre field. Directly ahead was a small field. Would the P-51 sideslip or would it simply fall on its wing and crash?

Jerry, knowing he had nothing to lose, said a quick prayer and then kicked the rudder left and pulled his stick to the right. The P-51 shuddered as it stood on its left wing and then settled into the small field as smoothly as the Taylorcraft back in Indiana.

Much to Jerry's relief the two men running to his downed airplane were shouting "American! American!" as they reached him. They quickly helped him get out of the plane and took him to a nearby house. It was then he learned he had landed less than two miles from the front lines but in Allied territory (held by the United States or its allies).

Four days later he was back in England, where he was given a week's leave before being assigned to a new P-51 at his home squadron.

Jerry wrote Clarence to tell him how the little airport at Lynn had saved his life.

"When I told the guys back at the base what I had done," the letter said, "they told me I was nuts. They thought I simply was lucky enough to get into a small field where grass was heavy enough to slow me down. So, I had to prove my point. I took my new P-51 up to wring it out and told my squadron buddies to watch. I came halfway over the field to land, kicked my rudder left and my stick right, laid the P-51 on its side, and slipped my way to a perfect landing. I had no more doubters."

A second young man named Billy, a native of the Lynn area, also enlisted before the United States entered World War II. He had only four hours of instructional time and had not yet soloed when he received his orders to report for military duty the first week of August 1941.

"Clarence," he said, stopping by for his last visit before heading to a base in Colorado, "unless the Army feels otherwise, I plan on being a pilot. There's no doubt we're going to go to war with Hitler, and I want to fly. Wish me luck."

Clarence, Nick, and Max watched as Billy drove out of the driveway, looking over his shoulder as he waved. "I don't know," said Nick, more to himself than to either Clarence or Max. "I don't know. I'm not sure he's got the ability to make it as a pilot. We'll see."

Nick was right. Billy was washed out of the fighter pilot program and was transferred to bombers. Since he was five feet eight inches tall, the young Lynn man became a tail gunner on a B-17 bomber. He had eight trips into Europe without incident and was sure of four kills of enemy aircraft.

But number nine proved to be his last. The B-17 was attacked by two German fighters and exploded in midair, losing all hands on board, including Billy.

When Clarence received word of Billy's death, he flew the American flag on the flagpole in the east yard of the Knight home at half staff in honor of the brave young man who wanted to be a pilot but didn't make it.

This is a P-51 fighter aircraft from World War II, the type Jerry sideslipped to land in a small field in France after being shot down by a German pilot.

HANGAR FLYING USA
Fighter Planes

If you flew the P-51 Mustang during the war, it was the greatest fighter airplane of World War II. If you flew the P-47 Thunderbolt or the P-38 Lightning during the war, they were the greatest fighter airplanes of World War II. That debate has not been settled even today.

The P-51 became the preeminent long-range escort fighter of the war. A P-51 was first used by the British Royal Air Force in 1940. The British and Americans enhanced the original model, and when the United States entered the war, the P-51 became the prime airplane to fly deep into enemy territory. The P-51s escorted the Eighth Air Force bombers, including the B-17, known as the "Flying Fortress." The P-51 D's most important feature was a rear fuselage reduced in height to allow for a bubble canopy (a clear cover over the cockpit that allowed the pilot a 360-degree view) and space for additional machine guns. It had a top airspeed of 437 miles per hour, making it outstanding in combat, especially against the famous German Bf 109. All models of the P-51 were built by North American Aviation, the same company that produced the famous B-25 "Mitchell" bomber.

The P-47, a fighter-bomber built by Republic Aviation Corporation, flew more than a half million missions and dropped around 132,000 tons of bombs. In all, 15,683 Thunderbolts rolled off the assembly line, more than any other fighter plane. Reliable, durable, and fast, the P-47 was used in nearly every location where American pilots fought. The P-47 logged almost one and a half million combat hours.

In May 1942 Republic, headquartered in Farmingdale, New York, leased ground for a factory to build P-47s in Evansville, Indiana. The factory rolled out its first plane, named the Hoosier Spirit, *on September 20, 1942. By the time the war ended in 1945, the Evansville plant, with a high percentage of women employees, had produced 6,242 Thunderbolts.*

The P-38 was manufactured by Lockheed and its contractors in several plants across the United States during World War II. Like the Mustang and the Thunderbolt, the Lightning underwent several design modifications at the beginning of the war. Also, like the other two fighter planes that could boast at being the best, the P-38 was flown in all the war's major arenas—Europe, the South Pacific, and North Africa.

The P-38 was credited with downing more Japanese planes than any other plane. This fighter also logged more missions in the Mediterranean theater than any other type of fighter.

CHAPTER NINETEEN

Nighttime Landing

*Never let an airplane take you somewhere your
brain didn't get to five minutes earlier.*

Landing at night became quite an adventure at the Knight Airport at Lynn. Nick and Clarence tried it first when they had trouble on a flight home from Danville, Illinois.

Darkness was settling over the field, and Max, Minnie, and Virgil Jones, who was there working on his loudspeaking equipment, were getting worried. They had received a telephone call almost an hour before, saying the two men had made an emergency landing east of Indianapolis for fuel and would be there within the hour. Clarence had told his wife to station both trucks and an automobile at each end of the field to give them a bearing for landing. She tried to talk him into staying where he was, but Clarence assured her there would be no problem.

It was later learned that the place where Nick and Clarence had landed east of Indianapolis was a cow pasture on a farm that bordered U.S. 40 on the north side. The fuel gauge had shown a quarter tank of gasoline, plenty for the final fifty miles to Lynn. But it was faulty, and suddenly the engine coughed and stopped dead, the tank empty.

Nick saw a field to the left that looked big enough to get into so he quickly glided for it and landed without hitting anything. The plane rolled to a stop, and Clarence got out. He walked over to the nearby house and knocked on the door. The family was eating the evening meal, and a young boy came to answer the knock.

"Is your father here?" Clarence asked.

"Hey, Dad!" the boy yelled, "some man wants you."

Virgil Jones was a vital part of the airport at Lynn, Indiana. Virgil is pictured here at the workbench in his home, working on his shortwave radio. Max Knight took this photo in 1953 for the *Lynn Herald* weekly newspaper.

COURTESY OF MAX KNIGHT

The man got up from the table and went to the door. "I ain't buyin' nothing so go away," he growled at Clarence.

"I'm not a salesman," Clarence answered. "My friend and I ran out of gasoline, and we wondered if we might get some from that tank out by the barn. We will gladly pay you whatever you say."

"If you are headed east, you just passed two gas stations," the man continued to growl. "If you are headed west, it's only a mile to another station. Kinda dumb to run out of gas."

"I'm sorry," said Clarence, "I should have explained. We are in an airplane and landed in your field over there. Our gas gauge malfunctioned."

"You're what?" the farmer exclaimed. "You're where?" He yelled again. "My God, man!" he continued to yell, "I got forty head of cattle in that field. How many did you kill?"

"None," answered Clarence, trying to keep his voice even to calm down the uptight farmer. "In fact, we did not know there were any cattle in the field until I got out of the plane to walk up here."

The farmer hurried out the back door of his home, saw the plane sitting in his field, and shook his head. "I've lived here for twenty-seven years. I've had cars and trucks and motorcycles and even people on bicycles stop here for a little bit of everything, but this is the first time I've ever been visited by an airplane. My goodness, what is the world comin' to?"

Without another word the farmer walked to a nearby shed and got two five-gallon gasoline cans. He handed one to Clarence and walked over to the bright red overhead tank. He quickly filled the two cans and walked with Clarence to the plane. Nick greeted him, and by now the farmer was over his shock and more relaxed.

"You the pilot?" he asked.

"Yes," said Nick. "My name's Myron Nicholson. We really thank you for helping us out. The gauge on the plane is faulty, and we thought we had plenty of gas to make it back to our airport north of Richmond."

"Oh," said the farmer. "You live north of Richmond? I got a son livin' at Modoc. That near you?"

"Only some ten miles west of us," Clarence answered.

"Wait 'til I tell him about this," the farmer chuckled. "He won't believe it."

After one more trip from the gas tank with another ten gallons, Clarence paid the farmer, shook hands with him, and started to get in the plane.

"Hold it a second," the farmer called out. "I'll go get the two boys, and we'll herd my cattle over to the fence so you won't hit one of 'em when you take off."

"While you are doing that," Clarence said to the farmer, "would you mind if I called home so we can have lights set up to give us enough light to land? I'll pay you for the call."

By this time the farmer was as congenial a person as you could find, and he told Clarence to go ahead. When Clarence finished the telephone call to Minnie, he left a dollar bill lying on the table.

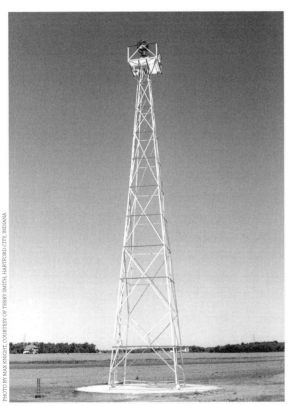

Beacon lights such as the one pictured here composed the highway for aviators in the 1930s. This beacon light has been preserved by Terry Smith of Hartford City, Indiana.

PHOTO BY MAX KNIGHT, COURTESY OF TERRY SMITH, HARTFORD CITY, INDIANA

Nick had the Taylorcraft warming up when Clarence waved at the farmer and crawled into the plane. In moments they were in the air and headed east. Everything below was black except for the twinkling lights from towns and farms.

Beacon lights were stationed every fifteen or so miles along U.S. 40 from Indianapolis to Richmond and on to Dayton, Ohio, and Nick aimed at the Nixon Airport light at Richmond. It was amazing how far those lights would shine as they constantly rotated from dusk until dawn. Pilots called them the highway of the sky.

At the Lynn Airport, Max, Virgil, and a man who worked for Clarence, Ralph Polley, followed Minnie's instructions as relayed from her husband. Clarence said to put one vehicle at the end of the field facing the same direction as the wind was blowing and two vehicles at the other end for them to pass over. Ralph drove the bigger truck to the south end of the small runway, turned it around, backed it to the fence and turned on the headlights. Max got in the pickup truck, turned on the lights, and parked it fifty feet to the east of the runway. Virgil positioned the automobile fifty feet to the west, closer to the hangar, and also turned on the lights.

It seemed like an eternity but actually was only fifteen minutes later when Max yelled to his mother, "I hear the plane! They're coming!"

Nick came in over the field to check out the lighting, turned the plane into the wind, dropped in between the pickup truck and automobile, and made a perfect landing dead center of the runway. He rolled to a stop, cut the engine, and opened the door. "Piece of cake!" he said to Virgil.

Night landings took place several times throughout the years. Max was involved once on a night flight returning from Middletown, Ohio. The two pilots, Nick and Max, had been to the Aeronca factory and had been forced to wait longer than expected while the finishing touches were put on the part that was needed.

"We should be okay," Nick said as they took off and headed west. "After that time we got caught in fog, I don't trust this going from a low level like Middletown, but it looks good right now."

Nick was flying at 3,000 feet and both enjoyed a beautiful sunset as Nick turned northwest to aim at the airport.

"Looks like clouds ahead," he yelled to Max. "I'm going to drop down a little and stay under them."

After dropping to 2,000 feet, Nick realized it would not have been necessary, as the clouds were well above them. But, as he said, "Better be safe than sorry."

Max was amazed at how quickly darkness set in as the clouds formed a dark cover above.

"Don't worry," Nick said, knowing the fourteen-year-old boy at his side had never landed after dark before. "Clarence will have lights for us."

He was right. When the plane had not arrived at sunset, Clarence stationed the two trucks and car at each end of the field, serving as landing lights in case they were needed. Clarence stayed with one truck, Ralph Polley sat in the second truck, and Minnie was in the car. When Clarence heard the plane in the distance he turned on his lights, and the other two followed.

Nick turned the plane into position to land, looked over at Max, and said, "You might as well learn now. Take it in."

Max later admitted he was scared as he came in over the lighted trucks, touched down midway across the field, and rolled to a stop well short of the end of the runway. In fact, as he taxied the aircraft to the hangar, he realized sweat was pouring off his brow. This would not have been unusual in August since there was no air conditioning in the Taylorcraft. However, this was November, and it was 44 degrees outside the plane.

HANGAR FLYING USA
Highway of the Sky

The transcontinental airway of the 1920s and 1930s was a network of beacon lights placed on towers and spaced ten to twenty-five miles apart across the United States. By 1933, 1,500 beacon lights lit up 18,000 miles of airspace across the country. When flying at night a pilot was never out of range of a beacon light, as each projected light for forty miles. The towers also housed course lights, with red lights if no airfield was nearby and green if there was an airfield adjacent to the beacon. This is how pilots knew where to make emergency landings if necessary. In addition, the beacons helped pilots know where they were because the lights for each tower flashed in a sequence unique to that tower so that pilots could match each beacon's location in a printed guide.

Clarence, riding with Nick, had the opportunity to follow the lights from Indianapolis to Richmond on two different occasions. He was amazed at how they seemed to actually stretch out in a highway of lights guiding pilots, not only for accuracy of distance but also of height.

The U.S. Post Office first began installing the beacons in 1923 to enable planes carrying the mail to fly at night. Regularly scheduled night service started July 1, 1924. Airmail could cross the nation in twenty-nine hours eastbound and in thirty-four hours westbound. In fall 1924 lights extended from Rock Springs, Wyoming, to Cleveland, Ohio, and by summer 1925, the lights extended to New York. After the post office contracted out its mail service, the responsibility for the transcontinental airmail route was turned over to the newly formed Airways Division of the Bureau of Lighthouses. This division continued to develop the "highway of the sky."

The Pitcairn Mailwing, Douglas M-2, and Ford Tri-Motor were widely used for airmail service during the second half of the 1920s. An open-cockpit plane that resembled fighters, the Mailwing was used on shorter routes, such as New York to Atlanta. The M-2 was larger, could carry up to one thousand pounds, and could be converted to carry two passengers. M-2s flew routes from Los Angeles to Salt Lake City and from Chicago to New York. The Ford Tri-Motor, used by several airlines by 1930, could deliver mail over long distances, such as the route flown by Transcontinental and Western Air (TWA) from New York to Kansas City to Los Angeles.

No matter how good the planes were, however, it would have been impossible for airmail delivery to be effective without beacon lights. Night flying was a must if deliveries were to be made in a more timely fashion than land routes alone allowed.

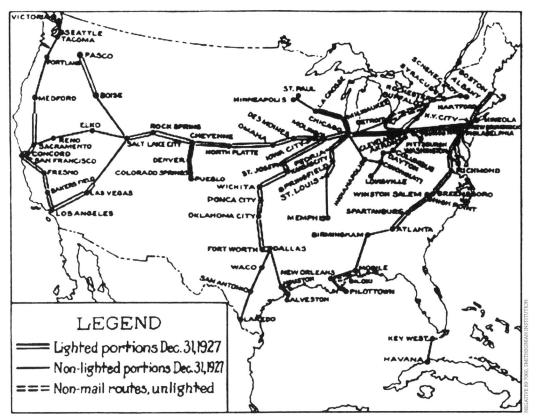

This map, labeled "U.S. Airways as of December 31, 1927," shows the sections of the airmail route that were lighted at the end of 1927.

CHAPTER TWENTY

Sunday Afternoon Air Shows

Good judgment comes from experience.
Unfortunately, experience often comes from bad judgment.

It was amazing the number of people who would park at the north end of the airport and spend Sunday afternoons watching the planes take off and land. Late in the summer of 1941, Clarence decided to put on some kind of show, adding to the fun of the day.

Virgil Jones provided the loudspeaker system for the airport on weekends and between announcements played records. The mid-1930s to late 1940s were known as the Big Band Era, and Virgil had all the great records of the day.

The song swinging out over the loudspeakers on this hot Sunday afternoon in August was Glenn Miller's newest hit, "Chattanooga Choo Choo." One couple, parked at the north end of the parking lot, was outside the car and dancing to the orchestra beat.

Clarence, who had been standing by the soft-drink cooler, hurried over to three pilots sitting in front of the hangar and said he had an idea.

"Let's take a door off the Taylorcraft and have Virgil turn up the volume full force. You guys fly low over the airport so that you can hear the music and move the Taylorcraft to its beat. The crowd will love it. What do you say?"

"I'm willing to try," Frank Baxter answered.

"Sure," chimed in his brother Kelvin, better known as "K," "let's give it a go."

"Count me in," said Eugene (Bus) Stegall. He had earlier thrilled the crowd with a low pass over the field in his Driggs Dart. This was a low-wing monoplane, quite different from other aircraft at the Knight Airport at Lynn. It had a 40-horsepower Szekely engine that gave off a loud, whining roar as it swept over the field.

Frank took off first, and Clarence explained to the crowd what he was going to do. Most visitors got out of their cars so they could see better. Frank headed into a northeast wind, and as he came in over the field at no more than fifty feet off the ground he moved the tail of the plane in rhythm to the music. As he passed overhead the crowd applauded. Frank made two more passes and then landed.

K crawled in the plane when Frank taxied it to the hangar, and off he went. Knowing the two brothers were rivals when it came to flying, Clarence wondered what K would do. He soon found out.

As the Taylorcraft came over the south end of the field, K started his rhythm pattern up and down instead of fishtailing it like his brother. It reminded Max of a fish swimming upstream, except each time he dipped the plane, K stirred the dust of the runway. When he bounced the last time and zoomed over the parked cars, people were yelling and clapping. It was unlike anything they ever had seen before—daredevil flying at its best.

K landed and taxied to the hangar. Frank and Clarence walked out to the plane. K cut the engine and took the Coke Max brought out, downing half a bottle in one gulp. "Top that, little brother," K said to Frank with a grin, sliding out the cockpit door.

Frank did not say a word. He simply waited until K was clear of the door and climbed aboard.

"Frank," said Clarence, "don't do it. That's enough. It's been fun, but I don't want someone to get hurt."

"Spin the prop," Frank said to his brother.

"Now wait, Frank," K chimed in. "What are you gonna do?"

"Don't worry," Frank replied. "I'll do a couple rolls and call it quits."

"Okay, nothing more," Clarence said, backing away.

Frank took off and first performed a quick wingover, turning while climbing into a near stall, then continuing to completely change directions while falling. Next, he zoomed low over the field to the roar of the crowd. Climbing again, he headed north from the airport a mile or so, did another wingover, and headed back toward the airport, now flying at a safe altitude for rolling the plane.

Frank rolled the plane twice as he said he would do and then climbed even higher as he headed back north a second time. This time as he roared over the field, Frank snapped the rudder left, turned the wheel right and then quickly back, causing the Taylorcraft to snap roll. Taylorcraft airplanes are not built to snap roll, but this one did. A snap roll is similar to a regular roll in that it is a horizontal spin; however, it is a rotation of the airplane with one wing stalled. It is dangerous in a plane built for aerobatics. It is foolhardy in one that is not.

Clarence let out a yell, "Those wings can't take that! Get that plane down here!" He was furious.

Frank landed safely, taxied the plane to the hangar, and, although the crowd gave him a roaring cheer, got the biggest chewing out of his life from the airport owner. The wings had stayed on, and Frank had landed safely. But the right strut wire that gives the wing its only upward support was hanging loose, dragging on the ground when the plane rolled to a halt. There was no way that wing could have stayed on without that wire. But it did.

Bus knew how upset Clarence was over the incident, so he begged off his turn at stunt flying. Nevertheless, as he took off for the Nixon Airport at Richmond in his Dart, he again buzzed the crowd to the delight of all present.

Dogfights, aerial battles with two or more planes, also added to the weekend fun, and the pilots loved it. That is, all the pilots loved it except one. Although he was one of the best pilots at the airport, Marion (Curly) Kennedy was by far the most cautious. Curly did not believe in wild maneuvers that could prove fatal. His favorite remark was, "Your first mistake can be your last mistake."

Max and Curly flew down to the Richmond Airport to borrow a certain wrench Curly needed to work on Nick's Great Lakes Trainer airplane. Curly not only flew quite often, but he also was the only mechanic Clarence employed to take care of the airplane engines.

As the two took off southwest from the Richmond Airport, Curly was flying. It was a typical spring day with the sun shining bright, the green of shooting corn starting to show against the dark ground below. To their left the shimmering waters of We-Hi Lake highlighted the entrance to the town of Cambridge City.

Eugene "Bus" Stegall is shown here with the Driggs Dart he flew into the Lynn Airport on two occasions and used in the Sunday air show mentioned in this chapter.

"Beautiful," Max said to Curly, and the pilot nodded his head.

Curly had a soft voice and was hard to understand above the roar of the plane, but as they turned north in the direction of Lynn he pointed toward U.S. Highway 27 off to the right and said, "Looks like an accident."

As Curly circled over the highway it was apparent a truck had smashed into the back end of a hay wagon. They went around a second time, and it appeared no one was injured so Curly leveled out and headed for the airport.

Both were enjoying the beautiful day as they passed over Fountain City and turned slightly northeast, knowing the approach to the field would be north to south in order to head into the light summer breeze.

As they neared the field Curly spotted another plane taking off in their direction. He instantly recognized it as belonging to Frank, and he knew immediately the pilot wanted to dogfight.

"Hang on!" yelled Curly, "I'm going in downwind. I'm not going to dogfight Frank Baxter under any conditions."

And that is what he did. He landed downwind, something pilots never do unless it is an emergency. Curly considered this an emergency.

Max wanted to fly with someone when they were entering into a dogfight, but Clarence said no. "Too dangerous," he told his son.

"And he's right," added Curly. "Let those nuts kill themselves up there. If they want to dogfight, they should join the Air Corps."

HANGAR FLYING USA
Cal Rodgers's Cross-continental Flight

Trying to make a name as a pilot by putting on Sunday afternoon aerial shows was common during the Golden Age of Flight. Greats like Jimmy Doolittle did it. Women pilots got into the act as well, including two of the most famous, Bessie Coleman, the first African American female pilot, and Katherine Stinson, the first female airmail carrier in America who also was a stunt pilot from 1913 until 1920. Other pilots used endurance flights, as in the case of Charles Lindbergh and his solo flight across the Atlantic Ocean. But the most unusual flight to earn fame may well have been made by Calbraith Perry (Cal) Rodgers, flying a Wright EX biplane named the Vin Fiz.

Rodgers learned to fly at the Wright School of Aviation in Dayton, Ohio, in June 1911. That year, William Randolph Hearst was offering $50,000 to the first pilot to fly across the United States within thirty days. Rodgers talked the Armour Company into sponsoring his cross-continental flight attempt as a promotion for its new grape soft drink, Vin Fiz. Just three months after his first flying lesson, on September 17, 1911, he took off from Long Island, New York, and headed west determined to win the Hearst prize.

Flying years before beacon lights were installed, Rodgers followed the train tracks westward. The tracks were not only a route to follow but also carried his wife, mother, two mechanics, and others who were traveling by train to serve as his crew. When he left New York, Rodgers also took a train car full of spare parts for the EX.

During his journey the young pilot made approximately seventy stops, crashed at least sixteen times, and ended the flight with a broken ankle. It took him forty-nine days to make the trip, missing the deadline Hearst had set by nineteen days. He was actually in the air eighty-two hours, and his air speed averaged fifty-one miles per hour.

Nearly five months later, a Wright Model B that Rodgers was test-flying crashed into the surf at Long Beach, California. Rodgers was dead at age thirty-three on April 3, 1912.

COURTESY OF DEAN BUNCE, LOSANTVILLE, INDIANA

Cal Rodgers signs autographs near Huntington, Indiana, one of the sites where he landed during his cross-country flight in the *Vin Fiz.*

CHAPTER TWENTY-ONE

Close Calls

That white thing up there is called a cloud. It is harmless unless another aircraft is at your level going the opposite direction.

Being ready for an emergency is vital in flying. Max learned this lesson early. Max was at the Nixon Airport west of Richmond one day. Richmond pilot Bob McDaniels wanted to fly a J-3 Piper Cub after the engine had been reconditioned. Max was standing near the hangar when Bob walked out and asked Max if he wanted to come along.

There was a low blanket of clouds, and at 3,000 feet Bob saw a big hole and flew through it to emerge on top. Suddenly they had gone from a cloud-covered day to the brilliance of an open blue sky with the clouds below them.

"They look like you could land on top of them!" Max yelled to the pilot.

"Don't try it," laughed Bob. "It won't work. If you want to fly a few minutes, take over."

Max did so and continued to fly eastward, dipping down until the plane was flirting with the wispy clouds and then lifting back into the clear sky.

After some ten minutes, Bob called out, "That was great, but we better head back. I'll take it."

Max let go of the stick and rudder bars and leaned back to enjoy going down through an opening in the clouds and the beautiful view in each direction.

Bob saw an opening to his left and headed for it. He started his descent by circling in the opening and in moments broke out below the clouds.

Suddenly a severe rush of air hit the airplane and hurled it upside down. Bob quickly shoved the stick forward and righted the plane.

"What happened?" Max yelled.

"Look," Bob said, pointing westward.

Disappearing in the distance was a huge airliner. Its slipstream, the stream of air driven backward by the propeller and causing reduced air pressure and forward suction directly behind the airliner, had been so strong it flipped the Cub over without the pilot ever knowing how close the two planes came to crashing into each other.

"Why in the world would he be flying this low?" Bob yelled as he turned into his pattern to land. "I'm sure no airliner is allowed below 5,000 feet."

Although the pilot made inquiries by telephone to the airport at Dayton, Ohio, he was never able to identify the airliner or find out why it was flying at such a low altitude.

Max ran into another unusual situation a couple months after the airliner episode. He knew his cousin Bud MacDonald was flying in from Muncie some time after noon. He found an excuse to head home from school on this beautiful October day so they could go for a spin.

The trees were gorgeous as the two pilots headed south from the airport and banked to the east, flying toward the Ohio line. The fuel gauge, which was a wire that stuck out the top of the tank in front of the windshield, showed a full tank. The 40-horsepower Taylorcraft was purring as smoothly as a cat rolling in catnip, and all was right with the world.

Max was flying and leveled out at 2,000 feet, heading toward a series of small lakes south of Greenville, Ohio. They sparkled in the sunlight as the plane circled over them. In fact, Max made two passes before heading back west.

"I'm supposed to be in school," Max said to his companion, "So let's go visit Spartanburg."

His cousin took over the controls and headed for the small town a couple miles across the state line in Indiana. When he spotted the school at the south end of town he started dropping lower. He circled the school at two hundred feet, and both pilots could see students looking out the windows as the plane flew by.

"Make a close pass," Max yelled to his cousin. As they flew no more than one hundred feet off the ground, Max waved at his fellow students, and they waved back.

"Let's climb," Max told his cousin. Bud started a slow circle upward, topping out at 8,000 feet.

"Wow!" Max called out to Bud. "This is beautiful."

At that moment the Taylorcraft engine quit cold. Bud exclaimed, "What in the world?"

Max said, "I don't know, but we got glide distance to the airport."

"Then you take over," Bud answered, taking his hands off the wheel. "If we crash, you take the blame. I don't want Clarence mad at me."

As Max took hold of the wheel he glanced at the fuel gauge wire in front of him and saw it was flat against the cowling.

"We're out of gas," Max said, pointing to the cowling. "That wire must have been stuck when we took off."

As the two young pilots were talking, Max was gliding toward the Knight Airport at Lynn, which was eight miles away. In moments it was in view, but Max had only one shot at landing in the small field. It would be dead stick and no second chance. It was something he had never done before.

As the airplane approached the field, Max suddenly realized how little it was. The plane came in over the edge of the runway a little high for safety, so Max put it into a slip to quickly drop lower and touched down halfway across the field.

By the time they rolled to a stop Clarence was there in his pickup truck to find out what had happened. When he realized the outdated fuel gauge had been the culprit, it took only two days for the owner of the Lynn Airport to contact Everett (Coxey) Cox at Winchester and purchase a 50-horsepower Taylorcraft with a fuel gauge on the dashboard.

Only one time during the years the Lynn Airport was in operation did one of Clarence's planes receive damage to a wing. The Waco 10 was notorious for ground looping after a successful landing. Ground looping means that after the plane lands on the runway and is rolling to a stop, it suddenly veers off to either the right or left and spins around if not controlled.

Nick fought ground looping virtually every time he landed the Waco. It got to the point where it was routine to fight off the right or left circle without giving it much thought. But one Sunday afternoon while Nick was taking passengers for rides, it caught up with him.

A strong west wind was blowing across the runway and buffeted the plane as it approached the field. Nick was concentrating so hard on the landing that he eased off once the plane was on the ground—and he paid dearly for it. Nick leaned back to relax from the rather hard landing when, in an instant, the Waco veered to the right, and he could not stop it. As the plane made the sharp circle it tipped, and the end of the bottom right wing hit the ground. Damage was minimal, but it sure hurt Nick's pride.

Marion (Curly) Kennedy patched the wing. In less than an hour Nick was back in the air taking passengers on countryside rides.

HANGAR FLYING USA
Howard Hughes

There is a saying among pilots that fits when they talk of close calls or of losing a friend due to some unexpected event. It is this: "No pilot really dies until he or she is forgotten." The names of Jimmy Doolittle, Amelia Earhart, Charles Lindbergh, and Wiley Post will live forever in aviation lore. But pilots and millions of other people will also remember one other aviator's name, that of eccentric billionaire Howard Hughes.

Hughes was born in Texas in 1905. He possessed a great love of aviation from his teen years. Over the course of his lifetime he set several speed and long-distance records and also experienced several close calls. At eighteen Hughes inherited a substantial percent of his father's estate, including the Hughes Tool Company, and in 1932 he started Hughes Aircraft Company. At this company, he helped to design the H-1 Racer, the plane in which he began setting speed records.

In 1935, while setting the first record in the H-1 with a speed of 352 miles per hour, Hughes kept pushing for a higher speed until he ran out of gas and had to make an emergency landing. In an enhanced version of the plane, in 1937, Hughes set a transcontinental flight record, flying from California to New Jersey in under seven and a half hours. However, he nearly blacked out enroute when his oxygen mask failed.

Hughes helped finance the Lockheed Constellation, which, in 1944, he made famous by flying it nonstop across the country in just under seven hours, another new speed record. With its pressurized cabin, the Constellation flew up to 20,000 feet above ground level, giving its fifty-four passengers a comfortable ride.

During World War II, Hughes Aircraft created military airplanes. At this time, Hughes designed his most famous plane—an oversized wooden seaplane nicknamed the Spruce Goose, which measured 218 feet, 8 inches in length and had a wingspan of 319 feet, 11 inches. Its height was 79 feet, 3 3/8 inches, with a maximum takeoff weight of 400,000 pounds, making it larger by far than any plane of that era. Officially known as the H-4 Hercules, the Spruce Goose was created to fly troops and cargo. However, the plane was flown only one time, on November 2, 1947. Hughes was able to get the huge "flying boat" into the air and traveled roughly one mile in about a minute.

While building the Spruce Goose, Hughes also designed the XF-11, a two-engine, high-altitude reconnaissance plane. Hughes nearly died while flying the plane for its first test flight when an oil leak caused the plane to crash.

Hughes survived four crashes as a pilot. He was a daring aviator and received many trophies for his feats in both flying and airplane design. Ironically, Hughes died in 1976 as a passenger in a plane crash.

Howard Hughes, ca. 1930s. Hughes was an eccentric but brilliant billionaire whose first love was flying. He became known worldwide for setting speed records for flight, including an around-the-world record in 1938. Later he became famous for constructing the largest wooden plane ever built, the Spruce Goose.

CHAPTER TWENTY-TWO

Lake Fun and Fear

It's always a good idea to keep the pointy end going forward as much as possible.

Clarence owned a cottage on Chapman Lake near Warsaw in northern Indiana, and often he and Nick would fly there midweek for a couple days. Clarence had worked out a plan with Jack Disinger, a friend who lived at the same lake landing, to pick them up at the airport. The routine included a telephone call to let Jack know they were coming and then buzzing low over the lake neighbor's house to let him know they had arrived. When he heard the plane overhead Jack would drive his Dodge touring car to the airport. The airport was located one mile on a straight line north from the lake where Clarence had his cottage and two miles by road.

The owner of the Knight Airport at Lynn had called Jack early that morning and told him they would be arriving sometime after two o'clock in the afternoon. Jack said he would look for them and see them at the airport. However, the morning went more smoothly than expected, and Clarence and Nick were ready to leave an hour before they had planned to do so.

"No use in calling Jack again," Clarence said. "He'll hear us when we buzz his house."

Nick agreed, so the two men boarded the Taylorcraft, checked for incoming aircraft, and roared into the sky, turning toward Warsaw.

It was a beautiful day for a flight. The sun was brilliant at their backs as they cruised north-northwest from Lynn at 3,000 feet. Nick, as usual, went to sleep while Clarence flew the plane.

The flight took an hour and a half, and Clarence thoroughly enjoyed the view. There was Muncie off to the left, Hartford City to the right, and Huntington right in front of him. The airport owner had the Taylorcraft cruising at 90 miles per hour.

Clarence turned slightly west when he saw Huntington, and within minutes spotted Warsaw ahead and to his left. He knew he was on the money in heading for Chapman Lake.

As many times as Clarence made the trip he never got over seeing all the lakes in the Warsaw area. He knew there were at least one hundred lakes in Kosciusko County, a breathtaking sight from the air.

The airport owner poked Nick and told him to take over. They dropped lower as they neared Chapman Lake, and Clarence pointed and yelled out, "That's Jack down there in the 'double boat,'" referring to the special boat Jack used for fishing. "He's the only one on the lake who has one with a pole hook like that, so it has to be him."

"Let's give him a thrill," Nick answered, breaking into a grin.

Clarence knew what was coming so he nodded his head and hung on. Nick laid the Taylorcraft into a shallow dive and zoomed over Disinger's boat, missing it by some thirty feet. As they pulled up and looked back, Jack was getting off the floor of the boat where he had dived when the plane zoomed over. Both men roared with laughter as they headed for the airport. They had given Jack a couple moments he would never forget.

Nick landed on the east-west runway, taxied to the area designated for visiting planes to tie down, and came to a stop. Clarence looked at his watch. It was twenty minutes past one o'clock, an hour before they had planned to arrive.

The two men walked out to the roadway that passed the airport on the north side and waited. Twenty minutes went by.

"Guess it took him awhile to get back to shore," Nick said grinning.

Twenty more minutes went by with no Jack showing up.

"I sure hope he didn't have any trouble," said Clarence, looking again at his watch.

At that moment the Dodge turned the corner east of the airport and slowly approached where the two men were standing. Jack was driving no more than 15 miles per hour, looking straight ahead as he approached the driveway. When he got to the driveway, without ever slowing down, he turned to the open window on the side where Clarence and Nick were standing. He put his thumb up to his nose, dramatically waved his fingers at the two men three or four times, and continued driving down the road.

Clarence and Nick had to walk the two miles to the landing. When they got there, Jack was seated in a chair in the front yard of the Knight cottage sipping a cup of coffee. He had a smile on his face that would have made a Cheshire cat proud.

Amusement turned to terror two days later when Max, who had been staying at the lake with a friend, joined Nick in flying home to Lynn. This day, too, started in brilliant sunshine, and Nick decided to start for Lynn as soon as lunch was over. When they lifted off the ground and turned southeast, billowing clouds could be seen to the west, but they did not look like thunderheads.

Within thirty minutes, the weather changed drastically. Clouds soon covered the sky in front and to the west of their flight path. Nick was concerned.

As they approached Muncie Nick said, "I have half a notion to land and wait it out, but we are only fifteen minutes from home, and it looks like it will be longer than that before the front hits. Let's go on."

Nick was almost right. The two pilots could see Lynn directly in front of them, maybe five miles away, when the storm hit. The storm front caused the Taylorcraft to stand on its tail, and Nick fought the controls to bring the airplane back level. Lightning split the sky. Time and time again the lightning flashed dangerously close to the wings of the plane. Max helplessly watched the storm outside the window while Nick worked to keep the plane on an even keel. Once again a wind shear caused the plane to suddenly roll hard right, but, with sweat pouring off his face, Nick was able to level the plane.

"There's the airport!" Max yelled above the raging storm. "Can you land in this wind?"

"I don't know!" Nick yelled back.

At that moment a streak of lightning slashed in front of the plane. Nick and Max thought they had been hit. Again Nick leveled the wings as he approached the landing strip.

"We've got to use the east-west runway," Nick yelled, meaning once on the ground the plane still would be the entire length of the twenty-acre field from the hangar. "I don't know if it will stay upright if I'm able to get it down," he added, still yelling above the screaming wind.

"Okay!" he yelled again. "Hang on! Here we go!"

Nick turned the plane into the teeth of the wind, lined it on the east-west runway, and kept almost quarter power as he guided the Taylorcraft toward the runway. The only fortunate thing was lack of heavy rain. The wind was still furious, but the rain was little more than a heavy mist.

There was a farm at the eastern end of the runway, and Nick anticipated there might be a sudden downdraft, a downward current of air, over the farm buildings so he came in high. He was right. The bottom fell out of the plane for an instant. Had Nick not kept the plane high, there is no doubt it would have crashed into either the barn or the house.

Suddenly Max felt a jolt as the wheels touched the runway. To the great surprise of both pilots, on the ground the wind was greatly decreased. The plane rolled to a stop, and Max realized he was shaking.

At that moment Nick looked at his companion, grinned, and uttered his favorite saying when he had accomplished something virtually impossible to do: "A piece of cake!"

HANGAR FLYING USA
Aircraft Regulations

If Clarence and Nick had followed the tongue-in-cheek rules posted on the wall of the Lynn Airport (and reproduced at right), they would not have given Jack Disinger such a hard time. Written anonymously, the rules came from a list dedicated to pilots who flew the mail. Student pilot Jimmy Houser was the culprit who posted the rules, attaching them to the inside wall of the new hangar on the day it was dedicated.

At the time it was hilarious reading. Max especially liked rule 21. But in many cases, the rules made a lot of sense.

Jimmy Houser, who learned to fly in this Taylorcraft, was one of the first five to solo at the Lynn Airport.

Regulations for the Operation of Aircraft, January 1920

1. *Don't take the plane into the air unless you are satisfied it will fly.*
2. *Never leave the ground with the motor leaking.*
3. *Don't turn sharply when taxiing. Instead of turning sharp, have someone lift the tail off the ground.*
4. *In taking off, look at the ground and the air.*
5. *Never get out of a plane with the motor running until the pilot relieving you can reach the engine controls.*
6. *Pilots should carry hankies in a handy position to wipe off goggles.*
7. *Riding on the steps, wings, or tail of a plane is prohibited.*
8. *In case the engine fails on takeoff, land straight ahead regardless of obstacles.*
9. *No plane must taxi faster than a man can walk.*
10. *Never run motor so that blast will blow on other planes.*
11. *Learn to gauge altitude, especially on landing.*
12. *If you see another plane near you, get out of the way.*
13. *No two cadets should ever ride together in the same plane.*
14. *Do not trust altitude instruments.*
15. *Before you begin a landing glide, see that no planes are under you.*
16. *Hedge-hopping will not be tolerated.*
17. *No spins on back or tail slides will be indulged in as they unnecessarily strain the planes.*
18. *If flying against the wind and you wish to fly with the wind, don't make a sharp turn near the ground. You may crash.*
19. *Motors have been known to stop during a long glide. If pilot wishes to use motor for landing, he should open throttle.*
20. *Don't attempt to force plane onto ground with more than flying speed. The result is bouncing and ricocheting.*
21. *Pilots will not wear spurs while flying.*
22. *Do not use aeronautical gasoline in cars or motorcyles.*
23. *You must not take off or land closer than 50 feet to the hangar.*
24. *Never take a plane into the air until you are familiar with its controls and instruments.*
25. *If an emergency occurs while flying, land as soon as possible.*

CHAPTER TWENTY-THREE

Adding Spice to Flight

Keep looking around. There is always something you missed.

Since flying became as commonplace to Max as riding in an automobile, flying often became monotonous and boring. Anything to add spice to the flight was an added treat.

Max and his cousin from Muncie, Bud MacDonald, were flying in early spring and had stopped at the Nixon Airport at Richmond before heading back to Lynn. As they were ready to crawl back in their plane to take off, pilot Bob McDaniels pointed to the sky and said, "Go chase those geese."

Max looked up and saw a big V formation of geese heading southwest.

"Stay over the last goose in the back of the V, and they won't break formation," Bob said.

Max took off, and Bud again spotted the geese southwest of the airport. They worked the plane above and to the back of the V formation, reversing the throttle slowly to edge in over the goose bringing up the rear on the left side.

As the wing of the plane settled over the goose he kept looking toward the two pilots. Although they could not hear the bird, they could tell he was squawking at the top of his lungs.

Max dipped the wing lower and the goose dropped a couple feet but did not break formation. Max eased the plane toward the goose, but still the bird held tight to its position. Nothing short of actually hitting the bird with the wing of the plane was going to make it fall out of line. Max and Bud were sure if they had edged close enough and had the plane door open, they could have plucked the goose out of the air, and it still would not have broken formation.

Another interesting bird to fly around was a buzzard. These large birds catch air currents and sail round and round, seldom flapping their wings. To the surprise of Max and Bud, they would not shy away from an airplane.

The two young pilots were returning to Lynn from the Richmond Airport, laughing over the goose that refused to break formation. Bud was flying when Max saw five buzzards a quarter mile east of the airport.

"Look, Bud," he said, pointing eastward. "Those buzzards are circling over our woods. I wonder what they would do if we circled them."

Bud was a little concerned about moving in on the buzzards, as they were flying less than one hundred feet above the trees. "Okay, I'll circle them," he answered, "but I don't want to get too close. If one of those birds hits our propeller we will be in serious trouble."

Bud dropped the nose of the plane toward the buzzards and started his circle in the same direction the birds were floating. Both pilots could see the bright red heads of the birds watching the plane, but they did not change their routine of floating on the wind.

Bud increased the throttle and pulled the Taylorcraft up above the buzzards. He again started circling around them, this time in the opposite direction. Still the buzzards did not change their pattern. The birds continued to circle before one finally landed on a limb high in a tree in the woods. Soon all five were settled onto tree limbs, and Max and Bud landed.

When they got out of the plane, both pilots told Clarence what had happened. He had a ready answer.

"Geese fly in a V formation," said the airport owner, "so those at the rear can rest while the lead goose breaks the forward wind. If you had made the lead goose break formation the entire V would have been broken. As it was they simply continued to follow the leader."

"As for the buzzards," he said with a laugh, "they are too lazy to let a little thing like an airplane stir them up."

A few days later, Max was flying with Lee Crossman when the veteran pilot got a huge surprise. They, too, were chasing geese. As usual the back goose would not break formation, but both pilots were laughing at the antics of the bird. After five minutes or so of pestering the goose, Lee, who was flying, turned away.

"Funny birds," Lee said as he glanced over at Max.

As mentioned earlier, flying became so routine to many who flew out of the Knight Airport at Lynn that any diversion added spice to the hours in the air. One such diversion was chasing red fox in nearby fields. In that era, red foxes overpopulated the farms of eastern Indiana and were a menace to chickens and small farm animals. Max enjoyed chasing the extremely fast-running animals, and on one particular spring day got a surprise as he was doing so.

Max was flying with Marion (Curly) Kennedy when they spotted a red fox running across an open field north of the airport. Curly agreed it was all right to chase it as long as Max did not get too low. Much to their surprise, as they dropped lower, two more red foxes suddenly joined the first one, and instead of chasing one they now had three. It was a beautiful sight as the sun reflected off the backs of the running animals, and their sure-footed twists and turns were fascinating to watch.

There was a problem, however. Max became so involved in the chase that he forgot he was flying, and the plane was getting slower and slower. Curly, who never raised his voice, said barely loud enough for Max to hear, "Might check your airspeed."

Max did and learned a lesson: Never get so involved in something outside the plane that you forget what you are doing inside the plane. It was a lesson Max would never forget.

Marion (Curly) Kennedy stands beside Clarence's first Taylorcraft at the Lynn Airport.

HANGAR FLYING USA
Colonel Bill Kelly

Bill Kelly and Max became close friends. But in the summer of 1941, Bill was eleven years old, and Max was fourteen. Their paths seldom crossed. Yet they shared a passion that would later bring them together.

Bill often walked the three miles from his home in Lynn to the Lynn Airport. At the end of the runway, he lay in the high grass at the side and dreamed that someday, maybe, he could ride in an airplane like those taking off. No one from the airport ever knew he was there.

In 1949 Bill joined the army and after basic training volunteered for airborne school. Two years later he graduated from Officer Candidate School. After making sixty-three parachute jumps, Bill went to the airfield at Fort Benning, Georgia, for a closer look at the planes. The commanding officer offered him a ride, and Bill was hooked immediately. Officer recruits were needed to fly both fixed-wing aircraft (airplanes) and rotor-wing aircraft (helicopters). Bill applied and was accepted.

During the next twenty-five years Bill had duty in Alaska, Libya, the Middle East, East Africa, Vietnam, Italy, and Germany, among other places. From 1967 to 1970 he was Aviation Advisor and Liaison Officer to all air forces for NATO (North Atlantic Treaty Organization). He retired with the rank of colonel and registered more than six thousand hours fixed wing and four thousand hours rotor wing in twenty-one different aircraft.

While on a mapping mission in Iran in 1956, Bill learned that the Shah of Iran, Mohammad Reza Pahlavi, had purchased two helicopters. The Shah, who was an excellent fixed-wing pilot, found out that Bill was a rated instructor, and Bill was asked to give the Shah flying lessons in one of his helicopters. The Shah was a natural; he soloed two weeks later.

Looking back Bill realized how fortunate and grateful he was that the Lynn Airport was only three miles away while he was growing up. It provided the inspiration to fulfill "an impossible dream" for an eleven-year-old orphan boy.

Lieutenant Colonel Bill Kelly, USAF retired, fell
in love with aviation while watching planes fly
at the Knight Airport at Lynn, Indiana.

CHAPTER TWENTY-FOUR

Colonel Roscoe Turner Visits

The probability of survival depends on the angle of arrival at landing.
A large angle of arrival equals a small probability of survival.

On a hot June afternoon Clarence and Nick were seated in the small restaurant at the Indianapolis Municipal Airport chatting with three other pilots when in walked one of the great aviators of that era, Colonel Roscoe Turner. One of the men knew Turner and asked him to join their group. He gladly did so, and in moments all six were telling stories of flying adventures, with Turner the dominant figure.

Surprisingly, when Clarence started talking about the huge success of his small airport on a country road in Indiana, Turner seemed fascinated. He asked Clarence several questions about how it was started and what plans he had for the future. In fact, Clarence and Turner did most of the talking for the next hour.

Then Turner looked at his huge pocket watch and said he had to be on his way. The men shook hands, and the famous pilot said, "I am sure we will meet again." Clarence thought there was little chance.

Imagine Clarence's surprise when the telephone rang on a Thursday evening two months later, and a voice said, "Colonel Turner here. If you haven't got other plans for Sunday afternoon, I will be flying from Indy to Columbus, Ohio, and thought I might stop and visit a few minutes."

Almost stuttering, Clarence answered, "Great, Colonel! Nothing is planned. We'll look forward to your visit."

"I should be there about two o'clock," said the famous pilot.

"Remember, Colonel," said Clarence. "We have a small field. It cannot handle a large airplane."

"No problem," Turner replied. "I'll be in a low-wing plane made especially for me. It can land on a dime and get a nickel's change."

As Clarence hung up he let out a war whoop. Max had rarely seen his dad more excited.

"We've got to spread the word," Clarence virtually danced as he talked. "This is the biggest thing ever to hit Lynn!" To Minnie he said, "In case you do not know, Colonel Roscoe Turner is the most famous speed pilot in the world. And he is coming to our airport! WOW!"

Clarence immediately started jotting down ways of letting the community know Turner would be there Sunday. First he called May Thomas, the Lynn telephone operator. She was the community news source for many people, and she readily agreed to spread the word.

Then he called a neighbor woman who practically lived on the party-line telephone. She was also more than willing to call everyone she knew.

"We do not have time to get posters made," said Clarence, "so call Virgil Jones and have him drive slowly through neighboring towns while using his loudspeaker to tell people about Colonel Turner. I'll call the newspaper and see if I can get a story at this late date."

The next twenty-four hours were spent in a flurry of activities as word of Turner's appearance at the Knight Airport at Lynn spread like wildfire. The big break came when the local radio station carried not only the announcement but also a vivid rundown of Turner's life.

Turner was a native of Mississippi, born on September 29, 1895. He enlisted in World War I as an ambulance driver but transferred to the air service as a balloon observer. He was discharged a first lieutenant. He later became a colonel in the Nevada National Guard.

After the war Turner and other barnstormers created the Roscoe Turner Flying Circus, in which Turner performed wing-walking stunts and parachute jumps. As barnstorming declined in the mid-1920s, Turner looked for another way to make a living. He got his first big break when he was hired as a stunt pilot for Hollywood movies. Notable in this part of his career was the daring and realistic combat flying he performed for Howard Hughes's great epic *Hell's Angels*. In 1929 Turner began racing planes and in the following decade set several speed records, including a few transcontinental speed records.

Turner was a striking character. He stood over six feet tall, featured a black, waxed mustache, and was famous for wearing military-type uniforms of his own design and for having flown for a time with a lion cub in his cockpit. The lion cub, named Gilmore, was a gimmick to promote the Gilmore Oil Company, which used a lion as its trademark. Many youth of the day looked up to Turner as a national hero.

Clarence's efforts proved successful. By noon on Sunday the parking lot that held fifty cars was full. Those who could not get into the parking lot pulled off the two-lane road for a quarter mile in each direction. Clarence had put out signs so that all traffic would park on the north side of the road, making entrance into the airport much easier.

Clarence was worried Turner might have changed his mind and would not show up when two o'clock in the afternoon rolled around and there was no sight of the famous

Roscoe Turner, 1968. Turner, a Hollywood stunt pilot, was famous for winning the Bendix Trophy in 1933 and three Thompson trophies, a feat never matched in the history of flying.

pilot. The airport owner paced back and forth in front of the hangar as he looked toward the western sky.

Max spotted the plane first and yelled to his dad while pointing southwest. When Turner reached the field he zoomed in low over the runway, did a pull up to the right that stood the plane on its tail, and rolled it no more than five hundred feet off the ground. It was a dangerous maneuver, but one the colonel called routine, and the crowd cheered.

The famous pilot continued to bring "oohs" and "ahhs" from the crowd as he pulled off three loops in a row, spun his plane eight times directly above the airport, and again zoomed in low enough to stir the dust as he roared over the field. He then headed into the wind and landed with precision.

Turner taxied his low-wing plane to the front of the hangar, turned the nose east so he could look left from his cockpit toward the crowd, and posed for pictures. He then held his hands up for silence and announced in a loud voice, "I am a speed merchant!" The crowd roared with delight.

Turner then stepped over the side of the plane and jumped to the ground. He shook hands with Clarence, ruffled Max's hair with his big hand, and waved to the crowd as he walked to the hangar. Max got him a Coke. He held it high as cameras continued to snap pictures.

The famous pilot was wearing a powder blue tweed coat, beige riding breeches, and a wide leather belt with a shoulder strap called a Sam Browne belt. He had shiny black boots, a white scarf around his neck, and sported a gold-and-crimson military helmet on his head. To the delight of those present he twirled his black mustache with his right hand as he waved to the crowd with his left hand.

Because Turner was famous and known as somewhat eccentric, Clarence was unsure how he would react to people at a small country airport. He need not have worried; the widely known pilot was friendly and gracious.

After signing autographs, talking with the people who gathered around, and posing for more pictures, Turner shook hands with Clarence once again and said he would pull off some more aerobatics before heading on to Columbus. He spent a little more than an hour at the airport.

Clarence realized there might be a problem. The plane Colonel Turner was flying was much faster and heavier than any aircraft that flew out of the Lynn Airport. He was concerned that the runway might not be long enough for the plane to get off the ground before it reached the fence at the south end of the field. He approached the honored guest to see if he had any suggestions.

The legendary pilot grinned at Clarence and said he had thought about that before landing. Getting a plane in a short field is no problem. Getting it out is a problem. But Turner had the answer.

"Clarence," he said, "if you will have five or six of those cars at the end of the runway move, I'll have some of the men back my plane out into the road, giving me an extra fifty feet for takeoff. Should work fine."

After the cars were moved, Turner started his plane, taxied it to the opening, and turned it to face south. Then he shut off the engine. Three volunteer men got hold of support pieces called struts on each side of the wing and two more stood on each side of the tail. Max, who was fourteen at the time, helped the men working the tail. They pulled the plane backward until the tail sat in the center of the gravel road that fronted the airport.

The celebrated pilot started the engine and signaled to the three men who were holding back on the struts, while Max and the other two men held the tail down. The pilot increased the throttle, and the men held on as long as they could. Suddenly the plane moved forward, and the men hit the ground as they let go. Turner shot down the short runway and leaped into the air well short of the fence. Clarence heaved a sigh of relief.

But the show was not over. The owner and operator of the well-known Roscoe Turner Flying Circus did aerobatics unlike anyone at the airport had ever seen. One stunt he performed is called the Immelmann. This maneuver is a half loop to inverted flight and then a half roll that results in horizontal upright flight in a reverse direction. The second maneuver he showed the crowd is known as an avalanche. This is a basic loop with a snap roll at the top of the loop that brings the plane on a level course. Both are extremely dangerous maneuvers but were done to perfection by the famous pilot.

On his last pass over the airport the daredevil pilot headed into the wind as he did three slow rolls to the roar of the crowd. They were still cheering as his plane disappeared from sight, heading east.

HANGAR FLYING USA

Air Racing

   Roscoe Turner was flamboyant but was also one of the greatest fliers in United States history. He won the highly coveted Thompson Trophy three times (1934, 1938, and 1939, the last year the race was held). The Thompson Trophy Race began in 1929 and, for daredevil pilots, immediately became their Indy 500 (known then as the International 500-Mile Sweepstakes). Held in either Cleveland, Ohio, or Los Angeles, California, it was the ultimate in airplane racing due to the speed of the planes on a closed course, flying around pylons for a specified number of laps. The

first three winners were Doug Davis, 1929; Charles Holman, 1930; and Lowell Bayles, 1931. The great Jimmy Doolittle won the race in 1932. Turner would have won the Thompson Trophy in 1933 but was disqualified when he accidentally missed a pylon at the finish. Jimmy Wedell won that year. In 1935 Harold Neumann won by just sixteen seconds. Michael Detroyat won the following year, and in 1937 Rudy Kling dived at the finish line to steal the win by five-tenths of a second. Turner holds the record for most number of wins in the decade that the Thompson race was held.

The Bendix Trophy Race, initiated in 1931, was a wild transcontinental race that normally started in Los Angeles, California, and ended in Cleveland, Ohio. Jimmy Doolittle won the first race in 1931, and James Haizlip won the 1932 race. In 1933 and 1936 the race ran from New York to Los Angeles. Turner set the transcontinental speed record as he won the 1933 event. Doug Davis captured the 1934 Bendix Trophy. In 1935 Turner lost the race to Ben Howard by twenty-three seconds. Frank Fuller Jr. took the prize in 1937 and 1939.

Famed women pilots also competed for the Bendix Trophy. Amelia Earhart finished fifth in the 1935 and 1936 races. Jacqueline Cochran placed third in 1937 and won the Bendix Trophy in 1938. The second-place finisher in 1936 was Laura Ingalls. That year, for the first time, an all-woman team, Louise Thaden and Blanche Noyes, won the race flying a Beechcraft Staggerwing. The women thought they had finished last in the race and landed well away from the cheering crowd. When a stream of men came pouring in their direction, the women wondered what was happening and were afraid they had done something wrong. Needless to say, they were elated to learn they had won the race. The Bendix race was suspended from 1940 through 1945, and 1949 was the last year in which propeller-driven planes competed.

With the major races in suspension due to the coming of World War II, Turner opened an aviation school in Indianapolis where he trained flight instructors, pilots, and mechanics. After the war, the Roscoe Turner Aeronautical Corporation continued the flight school and also sold and serviced aircraft through the 1960s.

In 1952 the U.S. Congress awarded Turner the Distinguished Flying Cross for his contributions to aviation. Turner died on June 23, 1970.

During the 1930s daredevil pilots competed to see how long planes could fly as well as how fast they could fly. Clarence rode in the back of this truck as it raced down the runway to send up supplies to a J-3 Piper Cub endurance plane in Muncie, Indiana. It was a dangerous job, but no accidents occurred during the flight in October 1939.

CHAPTER TWENTY-FIVE

Endurance Flight

Staying aloft in an airplane is joy.
Staying aloft for 535 hours questions the sanity of the pilots.

On October 23, 1939, at 6:43 p.m., 535 hours and 51 minutes after taking off, two young men took their place in aviation history. In a J-3 Piper Cub, powered by a Franklin 55-horsepower engine, Kelvin F. (K) Baxter and Robert A. (Bob) McDaniels completed a nearly 35,000-mile flight, a record for lightweight land planes.

McDaniels had set a previous endurance flight record with fellow pilot Russ Morris in 1938. They had kept a plane aloft for 130 hours over Richmond, Indiana. Al Heath served as the ground coordinator for that flight. However, their record was broken in August 1939, so McDaniels was determined to regain the record.

In 1939 McDaniels and Baxter decided to fly out of the Muncie Airport because the Singer Baking Company of Muncie was one of the principal sponsors of the flight. Singer had recently come out with a new line of bread, Sun Tan, so the plane was dubbed *Miss Sun Tan.*

Although the two men were known as daredevils when it came to flying, the purpose of the flight was to earn enough money so that both could go to instrument training school in the hope of becoming airline pilots. It worked. They both retired after many years of flying the huge passenger planes.

The endurance flight took place at the Muncie Airport, and Clarence and Max were part of that history. Clarence was part of the ground crew, and Max was the "gopher" when he could be at the airport. It was an experience neither Clarence nor Max ever forgot.

At designated times throughout the flight, ground crew chief Earl (Red) Luker drove a pickup truck down the runway as fast as it would go while his crew members, including Clarence, stood in the back of the open truck bed with the plane hovering only a few feet above them. A dangling rope would be hooked to gasoline cans, bags of food, or whatever was needed and hauled into the plane by one of the pilots.

Refueling and reprovisioning was a risky operation. On one occasion late in the flight, the engine misfired about thirty feet off the ground, and the plane had trouble getting airborne again. Clarence thought it all was over at that moment. During another refueling procedure, extreme turbulence caused the plane to nearly stall at only twenty feet up. Years later Clarence still wondered how the pilots ever kept the plane in the air and away from the speeding truck during these operations.

Fatigue was also a tremendous danger during the flight. As one man slept, the other flew the plane. These hours of isolation often caused the pilot to doze off. The feeling of isolation was overwhelming and something that McDaniels, at least, remembered vividly afterward.

Less dangerous but terribly wearing was the cramped space in the plane. The J-3 cabin was about twenty-five inches wide. Years later McDaniels described the flight as an awful ordeal and drew a visual picture by suggesting two people place chairs in an old-fashioned bathtub and live there for more than twenty-two days.

Clarence would not allow Max to ride in the pickup truck during refueling due to the extreme danger, but after school and on weekends, Max did a lot of running in between refueling trips. He carried empty gasoline cans, got rid of refuse the pilots dropped from the plane, and did whatever else needed to be done.

Max's first big thrill came when Nick asked Max if he would like to go up in the Taylor-craft and fly alongside McDaniels and Baxter. Of course the answer was yes, and soon they were in the air. The two endurance pilots enjoyed having friends fly alongside them, for it broke the monotony and loneliness of the flight. They started waving as soon as the Taylor-craft appeared on their left wing.

Max tried sign language but realized they did not understand what he was trying to say. However, he had written "Good Luck" on a piece of paper in large black letters, and when he held it against the window, both flyers gave a thumbs-up sign. Nick flew alongside the J-3 for ten minutes. Then with a wave good-bye, he broke off to return to the airport.

One other time during the nearly twenty-three days, Nick and Max took a similar trip alongside the endurance flyers. This time they could see fatigue in the pilots' faces.

Other people flew alongside the endurance pilots, too. This was one of the ways McDaniels and Baxter earned money with their flight. Pilots from the Muncie Airport took passengers on the flights for a fee. Baxter and McDaniels received a percentage from more than three hundred of these passenger flights. They also received money from the revenue of selling postcards of the pilots standing in front of *Miss Sun Tan*.

The endurance fliers experienced a few adventures on their long journey above Muncie. One of their biggest scares came near the end of the first week when a huge thunderstorm with lightning, high winds, and fog hit the Muncie area. Wind gusts were so strong that the wind sock on top of the Muncie Airport hangar was shredded. McDaniels described the blinding storm in a note he sent to the ground crew when they were trying to refuel. He stated that it "put a scare" in him he would "long remember."

500 HOURS GOAL OF TWO FLIERS

All's Well, Pair Report at End of Third Day.

Endurance Flyers Robert McDaniels and Kelvin Baxter hope to stay aloft 500 hours.

In a note dropped late Tuesday afternoon the young men told their ground crew that it is "500 hours or bust." Wednesday at 10:53 a. m. they completed the first 72 hours of their long flight and reported they were well and the engine was running smoothly. They found the air rough Wednesday.

"They installed a ventillator in their ship Tuesday afternoon," Earl Luker, head of their ground crew, said. "Air was stagnant in the front seat and they called for a ventilator and the tools to install it. We borrowed one from Clarence Knight, of Lynn, and they had it on the ship in a little more than an hour."

Flying since Sunday morning, McDaniels and Baxter must stay up more than 343 hours and 46 minutes to break the light airplane record held by the Moody brothers, Springfield, Ill. In their first attempt the flyers remained aloft 186 hours and 52 minutes, well over half the time of the Moodys.

MUNCIE (INDIANA) EVENING PRESS, OCTOBER 4, 1939

Stagnant air in the cockpit of the *Miss Sun Tan* became a problem, but was solved by Clarence. The endurance fliers needed a ventilator, and the Lynn Airport had one. Clarence brought the ventilator to Muncie, the fliers installed it in the plane, and it solved the problem. The newspaper report here tells part of this story.

Nearly one week into the flight, the two men were credited with saving the life of a farm family southwest of Muncie. At dawn on October 7, they had been flying their planned pattern when McDaniels spotted flames shooting from the front porch of a house. He zoomed low past the building but could see no one outside. So he dived the plane low over the house, both pilots howling frantically, in an effort to wake the family. On a subsequent pass they saw four people race out of the house. The homeowners, Mr. and Mrs. Carlisle Floyd, later told the Muncie newspapers that they and their two children had been sleeping and would have been trapped had they not heard the roar of the airplane engine.

A freak accident in the plane midway through the flight almost turned disastrous. The ground crew had sent up a half gallon of ice cream. After taking off the cardboard lid, Baxter tossed it out the side window. Within seconds the plane started vibrating.

Baxter opened the door, looked back, and saw that the lid had stuck on a wire on the rear of the plane. The vibration steadily worsened. At the plane's controls, McDaniels tried several maneuvers to dislodge the lid, but nothing worked.

Then Baxter thought of the bread from Singer. The baking company sponsor had sent up several loaves of bread so that the pilots would have plenty on hand for sandwiches. Instructing his partner to fly as level as possible, Baxter began throwing bread at the lid to knock it loose, but missed. He told the other pilot to fly faster. After a few more tries, the bread hit the carton lid, but the lid did not budge.

McDaniels called out, "K, it's now or never. This vibration is shaking us to pieces."

The next piece of bread hit the lid dead center, and it flew loose from the wire. The vibration stopped immediately.

When the pilots passed the goal of five hundred hours, the ground crew held a celebration and sent up a small cake to the pilots. McDaniels and Baxter decided to go for the absolute record for all planes, 673 hours. However, after 30 more hours the engine began knocking, and the men decided to land before their luck ran out. During the late afternoon of October 23, 1939, the pilots yelled down to the ground crew, "That's all. You're fired." Word spread quickly by radio and telephone that Baxter and McDaniels were coming in. The two men stayed in the air almost two more hours while media and spectators gathered.

The two pilots saw that each time they passed over the hangar area, more people were pouring in, so they circled the field a few more times. They decided to use the longest runway for safety's sake. As they cleared the end of the field and descended to about twenty feet, the engine suddenly quit. Unbeknownst to the spectators, the pilots landed dead stick. Had they decided to go around one more time they might well have crashed.

Max, Clarence, Red, and fellow ground crew member Eugene (Bus) Stegall were the first people to reach the plane. Red opened the door and helped the two fliers out. Bus and Red held the two men up as they wobbled forward. People cheered and crowded in as close as possible to see and take pictures of the two heroes.

The greatest honor for the two men came in Muncie a couple of days later. On hand to congratulate the pilots for their tremendous achievement was First Lady Eleanor Roosevelt. The wife of President Franklin D. Roosevelt traveled to Muncie October 25–26, 1939, to deliver a speech at the invitation of Muncie's Optimist Club. She also attended the dedication of Muncie's new Boys Club. Mrs. Roosevelt was a great booster of women in flying and, at one time, had worked toward becoming a pilot herself. So, when she heard about the endurance flight, she enthusiastically met with McDaniels and Baxter. Years later, McDaniels would tell his biographer that this was the highlight of the endurance flight for him.

A short time later the endurance flyers were also celebrated at a Muncie banquet sponsored by the Singer Baking Company. Clarence and Nick were guests, and Clarence was given the opportunity to publicly add his congratulations to the two men who had made lightweight airplane history when aviation was still quite young.

HANGAR FLYING USA
From Daredevil to Airline Pilot

A native of Muncie, Indiana, Bob McDaniels was an aviation pioneer as a teacher, barnstormer, and record-breaking endurance pilot. After his record-setting event with Kelvin Baxter, McDaniels flew as an Air Transport Command officer in World War II. He made ninety-seven round-trips across the Atlantic as a captain. Later, he flew routes across the Pacific during the Vietnam War as well.

McDaniels joined the staff of American Airlines and flew for thirty-four years, eventually earning the rank of senior captain. When he retired in 1974, McDaniels had achieved the pivotal mark of 30,000 accident-free hours flying for the airline.

McDaniels was a daredevil pilot in his early days, known by his middle initial "A." In 1937 he set a world record by spinning an airplane fifty-five turns. Max and Clarence, who were on hand in Richmond, Indiana, for the record attempt, witnessed as fellow pilots Bus Stegall and Russ Morris stood on the ground counting each turn.

In the mid-1960s, McDaniels returned to Richmond for a banquet honoring the men who had put the Indiana town on the map with their flying exploits. Each pilot in the room was asked to tell some story from his early days of flying. Max told of being with McDaniels when an airliner had flown so close to their small plane it had turned them upside down. McDaniels countered, "That was scary."

McDaniels was a member of the Experimental Aircraft Association, the OX-5 Club, and the Antique Airmen. For personal use, he flew a Canadian Jenny. McDaniels passed away in 1997 in Naperville, Illinois, but his name will be tied forever to Indiana pioneer aviation.

ARCHIVES AND SPECIAL COLLECTIONS, BALL STATE UNIVERSITY LIBRARIES

First Lady Eleanor Roosevelt, an airplane buff, congratulated the endurance flight record setters a couple of days after they landed. Kelvin Baxter is on the left and Bob McDaniels is on the right. Manager of the Nixon Airport at Richmond, Indiana, Bob had given Max his first flying lesson in 1936.

CHAPTER TWENTY-SIX

Epilogue

Learn from the mistakes of others.
You won't live long enough to make all of them yourself.

Aviation pioneers flew by the seat of their pants!

They flew airplanes with 40-horsepower engines. (Today you can find lawn mowers with as much horsepower.)

They put on a leather helmet and fur-lined goggles and climbed into an open cockpit to brave the elements and loved every minute of it.

They battled the winds seated in flimsy twenty-five-inch-wide cabins, giants of their time.

They marveled at pilots who could do aerobatics and then accomplished some on their own.

They looped, they spun, they hedge hopped, and they danced in the air, never worrying how those little planes withstood the pressure.

They landed in pasture fields that had been smoothed down with fence posts pulled behind pickup trucks.

They flew by feelings and not instruments or radios, nomads of the air.

They flew antiquated planes of World War I vintage and admired how they withstood the rigors of time.

They flew new planes as they came quickly along and felt comfort in the added power of bigger engines and refined aerodynamics.

They made constant strides that led to the jet age. They were some of the best.

Many of the aviation pilots who worked at or visited the Knight Airport at Lynn went on to bigger things in aviation:

Frank Baxter did not pursue a license for the airlines but remained a pilot his entire life.

Kelvin F. (K) Baxter earned his instrument rating and flew for Trans-World Airlines (TWA). Baxter retired to Florida and is now deceased.

Everett (Coxey) Cox operated the Cox Airport at Winchester his entire life, and Max flew from there on a number of occasions after the Lynn Airport closed. In 1921 Coxey purchased an airplane at Muncie and flew it to his home near Farmland, Indiana. He had been given no flying instruction other than how to start the engine. Coxey taxied the plane around the Muncie Airport for thirty minutes and then took off. When he reached

Farmland he glided in over his designated field to land but was not getting down as he approached the end of the field. So the self-instructed pilot pulled back on the stick, hopped over the fence, and landed in the next field without touching a thing. Like so many of the great pilots of his day, Coxey is also deceased.

Lee Crossman is the only pilot of those connected with the Lynn Airport who was reportedly killed during World War II. While mapping mountainous terrain in South America for the United States military, his plane went down. He did not survive the crash.

Al Heath, the senior pilot of those who flew out of the Nixon Airport at Richmond, joined Trans-Ocean Airlines after earning his instrument rating. He flew overseas schedules until his retirement to Houston, Texas. Heath is deceased.

L. B. (Tat) Lower first managed the Richmond Airport before becoming operator of the Rushville Airport where Clarence and Max took their first ride. Tat retired from airport management but kept flying until his death.

Bob McDaniels continued flying in his retirement from American Airlines. He taught flying to students until finally calling it quits at the age of seventy. He, too, has passed away.

Russ Morris joined Bob in flying for the airlines and was headquartered for years in Frankfurt, Germany. Like Bob, Morris became a full captain before his retirement. He has also passed away.

Myron (Nick) Nicholson was a nineteen-year-old teenager when he began giving flying lessons at the Lynn Airport. He taught others how to fly for an entire year before getting a limited commercial license and a permit to teach. During World War II he tested B-25 bombers out of Detroit, Michigan, and often buzzed Clarence, Minnie, and Max as he made his test runs. Diving at the house was a common practice. Many pilots did this to let Clarence know they were landing at the Lynn Airport. Nick continued this legacy after the airport closed with the B-25s, and on four occasions he caused a vibration that knocked bricks out of the chimney on top of the house. Clarence never told him. After the war Nick flew to all points of the world as chief pilot for the Mine Safety Appliances Company of Pittsburgh, Pennsylvania. He died of a heart attack at an early age.

Everett (Coxey) Cox (left) looks on as Dan Moulton works on Clarence's Waco 10 at the Muncie Airport in 1939.

L. B. (Tat) Lower, pictured here in 1939, took Clarence and Max on their first airplane ride at Rushville, Indiana, in 1936.

HANGAR FLYING USA
Flying Past 1941

Clarence Knight kept the promise he made to his wife Minnie when she agreed to his starting an airport. He could take off and fly with the best, but he promised to never learn how to land an airplane. Minnie believed that as long as he did not learn how to land, he would never go up by himself and have a fatal accident. Clarence did as she asked, and her words proved true. Clarence never flew again after the Lynn Airport closed in 1941. He died of a heart attack in 1945. Minnie passed away two months later.

As for Max, he flew strictly as a hobby until 1979, when he decided to hang it up. In his later years of flying he fell in love with helicopters and greatly enjoyed flying them whenever possible. However, every time he went up he thought of a statement his Richmond newspaper friend Ed Kaeuper made when he heard that Max had flown a helicopter. Ed loved flying but detested helicopters. His remark was, "Helicopters aren't made to fly. You need wings to fly. Try landing dead stick if you think I'm wrong."

Only one time did Max fly a twin-engine plane and that was during a trip to Kansas City. The plane, a Twin Beech, was a tremendous thrill to fly. And only once since flying in his father's Waco at the Lynn Airport did he again fly in an open-cockpit plane. It was a Stearman Model 75 biplane. The owner of the plane signaled to Max to take over the controls after they were in the air.

For a few minutes Max was transported back fifty years, flying once again as he had done in that bright red Waco 10, his helmet and goggles in place. But there was a difference. He did not need a cushion at his back or on the seat to see over the side of the plane. He needed only a handkerchief to wipe away the tears.

The years of flying, long gone, are like a dream. But they happened, and Max is a better man because they did.

Max Knight, 2005

Glossary

altimeter: An instrument that determines the elevation (height) of an aircraft by using measurements of air pressure.

avalanche: Stunt maneuver featuring a snap roll at the top of a loop that brings the plane on a level course.

barnstorming: An expression used by pilots in the early days for hauling passengers from a base not fixed or permanent.

biplane: A fixed-wing airplane with two wings mounted one above the other.

bubble canopy: A clear, bubble-shaped covering over the cockpit, designed to give the pilot a 360-degree view.

cowling: The cover housing an airplane's engine.

dive: A steep descent of an airplane toward the ground.

dogfight: An aerial battle between two or more planes.

downdraft: A downward current of air.

flat spin: A dangerous spin in which an airplane rotates on a level pitch rather than with the nose pointed downward.

floor stick: A device used by the pilot to control an airplane's movement up, down, left, or right.

fuselage: The body portion of an airplane that holds the pilot, passengers, and cargo.

ground looping: An uncontrollable, violent turn of an airplane on the ground that occurs during takeoff or landing.

hedge hopping: A maneuver in which an airplane flies almost at ground level, hopping over objects and often frightening people caught unaware.

high wing: Wing mounted above the body of an airplane.

Immelmann: A stunt maneuver that features a half loop to inverted flight, then a half roll that results in a horizontal upright flight in a reverse direction.

loop: A stunt maneuver in which an airplane flies in a vertical circle.

low wing: Wing mounted below the body of an airplane.

magneto: Device that generates electrical power to create combustion in an airplane engine.

monoplane: Aircraft with one pair of wings.

power dive: A dive in which the airplane descends quickly with full engine power.

propliner (aka prop airliner): A large passenger airplane powered by piston engines and driven by propellers.

Myron (Nick) Nicholson came within seconds of death when his Great Lakes Trainer, shown here, went into a flat spin over the Lynn Airport. A flat spin is very dangerous, spinning the plane on a level pitch rather than with the nose pointed downward. Flat spins can be impossible to recover from, and, so, are often fatal. Fortunately, a gust of wind saved Nick's life.

rip cord: The cord pulled to deploy a parachute during a jump.

roll: A maneuver in which an airplane spins on its axis while maintaining its horizontal direction.

rudder bars: Foot controls used by the pilot to operate an airplane's vertical tail surface.

sideslip: A maneuver in which the pilot slides the airplane sideways for rapid descent.

slipstream: The stream of air driven by the propeller toward the back of an airplane that causes reduced air pressure and forward suction immediately behind the airplane.

snap roll: A maneuver in which the airplane rotates in a horizontal spin with one wing stalled.

spin: A maneuver in which an airplane descends in a downward spiral.

stabilizer: The fixed horizontal part of an airplane's tail assembly that helps keep an airplane stable in flight.

stall: A sudden drop in altitude that occurs when an aircraft's speed has dropped below that required to maintain flight.

strut brace: A structural element used in providing support to the wings of an airplane.

three-point landing: A landing in which all of the airplane's wheels touch the ground at the same time.

trimotor: An airplane with three engines.

wind shear: A sharp shift in wind speed and direction occurring over a very short distance.

wingover: A maneuver in which an airplane enters a climbing turn until the plane nearly stalls; the airplane's nose is then allowed to fall while the turn continues, ultimately returning to flight in the opposite direction from which the maneuver was entered.

wing-walking: A stunt in which a person is fastened to a harness on the top wing of a biplane while the airplane is in flight and the pilot performs maneuvers.

Aircraft Manufacturers and Models

Aeronautical Corporation of America (Aeronca)
Founded in Cincinnati, Ohio.
1928–present

    Aeronca K

Aircraft Manufacturing Company (Airco)
Founded by George Holt Thomas in London, England.
1911–1920?

    De Havilland (DH)

Beech Aircraft Corporation
Founded by Walter and Olive Beech in Wichita,
    Kansas.
1932–present (now Hawker Beechcraft
    Corporation)

    Model 17 "Staggerwing"
    Model 18 "Twin Beech"

Boeing Airplane Company
Founded by William Boeing in Seattle,
    Washington, as Pacific Aero Products.
1916–present

    B-17 "Flying Fortress"

Brunner-Winkle Corporation
Founded by A. Brunner and William Winkle in
    Garden City, New York, as the Royal Aircraft
    Factory.
1926–1931

    "Bird" (CK)

The dean of eastern Indiana flying in the late 1930s was
Al Heath. This C. K. Kinner Bird was his favorite plane.

Consolidated Aircraft Corporation
Founded by Major Reuben Fleet in Buffalo, New York;
    sold to Vultee Aircraft Incorporated in 1941.
1923-1941

    Fleet biplane

Curtiss Aeroplane and Motor Company
Founded by Glenn Curtiss and Augustus Herring as
    the Herring-Curtiss Company.
1909–1929

    Canuck
    "Jenny"
    Model D
    Standard-Curtiss J-1

Curtiss-Wright Corporation
Founded when Curtiss Aeroplane and Motor
    Company and Wright Aeronautical merged.
1929–present

    Curtiss-Wright Pusher

Davis Aircraft Company
Founded by Walter C. Davis in Richmond, Indiana.
1929–1932

    D-1

Douglas Aircraft Company
Founded by Donald Douglas and David Davis in
    California as the Davis-Douglas Company.
1920–present (merged with Boeing in 1996)

    M-2

Driggs Aircraft Corporation
Founded by Ivan H. Driggs in Lansing, Michigan.
1927–1938

    Driggs Dart

Fairchild Aviation Corporation
Founded by Sherman Fairchild.
1934–present

    Model 24

Ford Motor Company
Founded by Henry Ford in Detroit, Michigan.
1903–present

     Tri-Motor 4-AT /"Tin Goose"

Great Lakes Aircraft Corporation
Founded in Cleveland, Ohio.
1935–1939

     Great Lakes Sport Trainer

Hughes Aircraft Company
Founded by Howard Hughes.
1932–present (merged and reorganized within
     Boeing and General Motors corporations in the
     late 1990s)

     H-1 Racer
     H-4 Hercules "Spruce Goose"
     XF-11

The Lockheed Company
Founded by Allan and Malcolm Loughead in
     San Francisco, California, as the Alco
     Hydro-Aeroplane Company.
1912–present (now Lockheed Martin)

     Constellation
     Explorer
     F-104 Starfighter
     F-117 Nighthawk
     Orion
     P-38 Lightning

Lockheed Martin Corporation
Formed when the Lockheed and Martin Marietta
     corporations merged.
1995–present

     F/A-22 Raptor

Messerschmitt, Incorporated
Founded by Willy Messerschmitt in Germany.
1938–1969

     Bf 109

North American Aviation
Founded by Clement Keys.
1928–present (merged with Boeing in 1996)

     B-25 "Mitchell"
     P-51 "Mustang"

Piper Aircraft Corporation
Founded by William T. Piper in Lock Haven,
     Pennsylvania
1937–present

     J-3 Piper Cub

Pitcairn Aircraft, Incorporated
Founded by Harold Pitcairn in Pennsylvania.
1926–1929

     PA-5 Mailwing

Republic Aviation Company
Founded when Seversky Aircraft elected new
     company president W. Wallace Kellett and
     changed its name.
1939–1965 (acquired by Fairchild Industries in 1965)

     P-47 Thunderbolt

Ryan Airlines
Founded by T. Claude Ryan and Benjamin Franklin
     Mahoney.
1926–1968 (acquired by Teledyne Technologies
     Incorporated in 1968)

     Ryan monoplane

Standard Aircraft Corporation
Founded by John Sloane as the Sloane Airplane
     Company.
1917–1928

     SJ-1

Stearman Aircraft Company
Founded by Lloyd Stearman in Venice, California.
1926–1929

     Model 75

Taylor Brothers Aircraft Company

Founded by C. Gilbert Taylor and Gordon Taylor in Rochester, New York.

1927–present (Taylorcraft Aviation Corporation in Alliance, Ohio, since 1935)

J-2 Taylor Cub

Taylorcraft

Travel Air Manufacturing Company

Founded by former employees of the Swallow Aircraft Manufacturing Company, including Lloyd Stearman, Walter Beech, and Clyde Cessna, in Wichita, Kansas.

1924–1929 (acquired by Curtiss-Wright Corporation in 1929)

Travel Air

WACO Aircraft Corporation

Founded as Weaver Aircraft Company in Lorain, Ohio, by George Weaver, Elwood Junkin, Clayton Bruckner, and Charles Meyers, and moved to Troy, Ohio, in 1923.

1920–1946

Waco 10

Waco F

Wilbur and Orville Wright

1903

Wright Flyer

The Wright Company

Founded by Wilbur and Orville Wright in New York.

1909–1929

Wright EX

Wright Model B

Acknowledgments

A sincere thank you goes to all the men and women who made this book possible. They lived or relived the Golden Age of Flying and left memories that have kept the wings level and the engine warm.

My safe flying award goes to M. Teresa Baer, editor of Family History Publications at the Indiana Historical Society Press, and her staff: editorial assistants Geneil Breeze and Rachel Popma and interns Evan Gaughan and Wendy L. Adams. Teresa's guiding hand got me through hours of flying in rough weather, and her encouragement kept this old pilot square to the runway.

Longtime pilot and friend Marvin Stohler earns my precision landing certificate for outstanding work in proofreading the manuscript and catching me in several wrong turns. Marvin is a walking encyclopedia on aviation, having built five airplanes from the ground up and restored several more. Since soloing at the age of sixteen in 1943, Marvin logged 3,500 hours as a pilot, served as manager of the Hagerstown Airport for many years, and is now retired from the Perfect Circle Division of the Dana Corporation after forty-two years in engineering and marketing services. I owe Marvin a great deal of credit for this book being accurately completed.

My first pilot flying permit goes to Dr. John Straw, curator of the Alexander M. Bracken Library at Ball State University in Muncie, Indiana. John came up with photos I had hunted for months and was gracious in opening his files for any that could be used. My second permit was earned by Frederick (Fritz) Morgenstern, longtime friend and pilot, who answered many questions with his knowledge of flying and library of books. It was Fritz who reminded me that, in the aviation world, pilots sitting around an airport telling stories are known to be "hangar flying." Therefore, a section titled "Hangar Flying USA" appears at the end of each chapter and contains additional information about significant airplanes, persons, or events important to the history of flight in the United States.

Sue King at the Morrisson-Reeves Library in Richmond receives my third flying permit for her warm reception to my search and for going the extra mile in getting what was needed. Computer whiz Bill Townsend earns my fourth flying permit for his splendid work in putting the book manuscript all together on disks. The aerobatics award goes to Steve Wieseke and his brilliant staff at Nettle Creek Colors, also in Hagerstown, for photography work above and beyond the call of duty. Photos taken in the 1930s spun their way through the clouds with remarkable clarity. A special thanks to Cinda Blevins for riding in the copilot seat.

Others soloed along the way: my wife, Mazella, for forwarding only vital telephone calls to me while I worked in the office; our son, Eric, for helping with computer problems; and especially our daughter, Teresa Jackson, for suggesting the Knight Airport at Lynn book idea to me in the first place.

List of Sources

Books

Ball, Edmund F. *Rambling Recollections of Flying and Flyers*. Muncie, IN: E. F. Ball, 1993.

Carl, Ann B. "WASPS." Chap. 5 in *A WASP Among Eagles: A Woman Military Test Pilot in World War II*. Washington, D.C.: Smithsonian Institute Press, 1999.

Knarr, Orv. *Middletown's Maverick Flyer*. Baltimore, MD: PublishAmerica, 2005.

Taylor, Michael John Haddrick. *Jane's Encyclopedia of Aviation*. Danbury, CT: Grolier Educational, 1980.

Wynn, Humphrey. *Desert Eagles*. Osceola, WI: Motorbooks International Publishers and Wholesalers, 1993.

Oral Histories

Kaeuper, Ed, and Max Knight. Notes taken of story told by Bob McDaniels at birthday party for Ed Rodefeld, fall 1965, Richmond, Indiana.

Kelly, Bill, and Max Knight. September 2006.

Meier, Joyce, and Max Knight. September 2006.

Stohler, Marvin, and Max Knight. 2005–2007.

Periodicals

(All Web sites were accessed between August 2006 and September 2007.)

Bennett, Pamela J., ed. "Aviation in Indiana." Special issue, *The Indiana Historian* (June 1998). http://www.statelib.lib.in.us/www/ihb/publications/aviationinindiana.pdf.

"Breaking Barriers in Space: Collins Is First Female Shuttle Commander." *Spaceport News*, July 9, 1999. http://www.nasa.gov/centers/kennedy/news/snews/spnews_toc.html.

Davisson, Budd. "High Wing vs. Low Wing." *Plane and Pilot*, February 2002.

Dorr, Robert F., and Fred L. Borch. "History in Blue: WWII Glider Pilot Was Aviation Legend." *ArmyTimes*, June 1, 2006. http://www.armytimes.com/legacy/rar/1-292308-1836458.php.

"Family in Burning House Awakened by Flyers Here," *Muncie Evening Press*, October 7, 1939.

Glines, C. V. "St. Petersburg Tampa Airboat Line: World's First Scheduled Airline Using Winged Aircraft." *Aviation History*, May 1997.

Hopkins, George E. "Transcontinental Air Transport, Inc." *American Heritage Magazine* 27, no. 1 (December 1975).

Howe, Robert F. "They Turned the Tide: Members of the Doolitle Raiders Celebrate the 60th Anniversary of the U.S. Answer to Pearl Harbor." *Smithsonian*, August 2002.

Morrow, Ben H., and K. W. Charles. "Cal Rodgers and the Vin Fiz." *Historic Aviation*, October 1969.

Mull, June. "First Lady Sees No Danger of Nation's Youth Becoming Communistic." *Muncie Morning Star*, October 26, 1939.

"No. 13 Out." *Time*, November 7, 1932.

"Obituaries: Raymond Kelly." *The Almanac Online*, October 15, 2003. http://www.almanacnews.com/morgue/2003/2003_10_15.obit.html.

Obituary for Robert A. McDaniels. Press release from Beildelhan-Kunsch Funeral Home, Naperville, IL. October 7, 1997.

O'Callaghan, Tim. "Historic Ford Airport 'Reopens' for Ford Motor Company Centennial." *The Ford Legend* 12, no. 2 (Fall 2003). http://www.hfha.org/fordairport.htm.

O'Leary, Michael. "Forgotten Racers: Mr. Wittmans's Bonzo." *Air Classics*, August 2003.

Orndorff, Bill. "Wrecks, Injuries, Plagued First Cross-Country Flight." *Hilltop Times Online*, September 11, 2003. http://hilltop.standard.net/story.asp?edition=119&storyid=3297.

Sheeley, Rachel E. "Dreams Took Wing in Richmond." *Richmond (IN) Palladium*, October 23, 1997.

Simonsen, Erik. "Historical Perspective: Howard Hughes, Aviation Legend." *Boeing Frontiers Online*, February 2005. http://www.boeing.com/news/frontiers/archive/2005/february/i_history.html.

Slutz, Theodore. "How He Came Back: E. Howard Cadle and the Cadle Tabernacle." *Traces of Indiana and Midwestern History* 17, no. 1 (Winter 2005).

Transport Canada. "Recent SeaRey Accidents." *Aviation Safety Ultralight and Balloon*, February 2000. http://www.tc.gc.ca/CivilAviation/systemSafety/newsletters/tp7317/2-00/menu.htm.

Vinarcik, Edward J. "Ford's Tri-Motor." *Advanced Materials and Processes* 161, no. 10 (October 2003).

"Youth's Problems Are 'Our Problems' First Lady Says," *Muncie Evening Press*, October 26, 1939.

Working Papers and Manuscripts

Hall, Donald. "Technical Preparation of the Airplane 'Spirit of St. Louis.'" Photocopy, National Advisory Committee for Aeronautics, Washington, D.C., 1927.

Hall, Jim. "Safety Recommendation." Photocopy, National Transportation Safety Board, Washington, D.C., 1997.

Kaske, Kristine L. "Fairchild Industries, Inc. Collection." Photocopy, National Air and Space Archives, Washington, D.C., 2003.

Roosevelt, Eleanor, to Amelia Earhart, January 18, 1933. George Palmer Putnam Collection of Amelia Earhart Papers. Purdue University Library.

Stegall, Eugene (Bus) "500 Hours or Bust." Eugene (Bus) Stegall Collection. Morrisson-Reeves Library, Richmond, IN.

Internet Sources

AcePilots. "Wiley Post." http://www.acepilots.com/post.html.

Aeronca, Inc. "Aeronca History." Magellan Aerospace Corporation. http://www.aeroncainc.com/history.html.

Air Transport Association. "The Airline Handbook— Online Version." http://www.members.airlines.org/about/d.aspx?nid=7946.

Allen, Russ. "The North American P-51 Mustang: World War Two's Most Prominent Air Superiority Fighter." Dr. D. Brendan Nagle's Homepage. http://www-rcf.usc.edu/~nagle/P51page.html.

Anderson, Nels. "Flying the Ford Trimotor." FlightSim.com. http://www.flightsim.com/cgi/kds?$=main/feature/ford.htm.

Arizona Aerospace Foundation. "WACO RNF." http://www.pimaair.org/Acftdatapics/Waco%20RNF.htm.

Arkansas Air Museum. "The Travel Air Company." http://www.arkairmuseum.org/exhibits/exhibit-travelair.php.

Atlanta Historical Museum. "Bessie Coleman, 1892–1926." http://www.bessiecoleman.com/.

Australian Parachute Federation. "Early History." http://www.apf.asn.au/history.aspx.

Aviation History Online Museum. http://www.aviation-history.com/.

Aviationweb déjà vu. "G-AJPI Fairchild 24R-46A Argus 3." http://avia-dejavu.net/photo%20G-AJPI.htm.

The Boeing Company. http://www.boeing.com/.

Century of Flight. http://www.century-of-flight.net/.

Charles A. and Anne Morrow Lindbergh Foundation. "Charles A. Lindbergh Biography." http://www.lindberghfoundation.org/history/calbio.html.

Charles Lindbergh, an American Aviator. http://www.charleslindbergh.com/.

Cleveland National Air Show. "History of the Cleveland National Air Races." http://www.clevelandairshow.com/press_room/natlairraces.htm.

Cole Palen's Old Rhinebeck Aerodrome. "Bird, Model CK." http://www.oldrhinebeck.org/collection/airplanes/bird.htm.

Cradle of Aviation Museum. "Brunner Winkle Bird." http://www.cradleofaviation.org/exhibits/golden_age/brunner_winkle/index.html.

Crawford Auto-Aviation Museum. "1929 Great Lakes 2T-1A Sport Trainer." http://www.wrhs.org/crawford/.

Curtiss-Wright Corporation. "Our History: The Spirit of Innovation." http://www.curtisswright.com/history.asp.

Dailey, Franklyn E., Jr. "Aircraft Endurance and Altitude Records: The GeeBee and Jimmy Doolittle Went for Speed." http://www.daileyint.com/flying/flywara.htm.

Davis Monoplanes. http://www.davismonoplane.com/.

Doolittle, James H. "Report on the Aerial Bombing of Japan." June 5, 1942. http://www.doolittleraider.com/interviews.htm.

EAA AirVenture Museum. http://www.airventuremuseum.org/.

Early Birds of Aviation. http://www.earlyaviators.com/.

Eichhorn, Guenther. "Aerobatics Figures." International Aerobatic Club. http://www.iac.org/begin/figures.html.

Eighth Air Force Historical Society of Minnesota. "Aircraft." http://www.8thmn.org/aircraft.htm.

Evansville Regional Airport. "History." http://www.evvairport.com/history/.

Evergreen Aviation Museum. "Boeing Stearman Model 75." http://www.sprucegoose.org/aircraft_artifacts/ Aircraft/WWII/Stearman.htm.

Experimental Aircraft Association. "1929 Brunner-Winkle 'Bird,' BK." http://www.eaa231.org/.

Experimental Aircraft Association. "Henry Ford, Ford Motor Company Founder and Aviation Pioneer." EAA's Countdown to Kitty Hawk. Adapted from the National Aviation Hall of Fame. http://www.countdowntokittyhawk.com/sponsors/ford/henryford.html.

FlightDeck. "The Hangar: Curtiss Seagull." Discovery Channel Canada and the Canada Aviation Museum. http://www.exn.ca/FlightDeck/Aircraft/Hangar2.cfm?StoryName=Curtiss%20Seagull.

Fly TWA Historical Site. http://www.flytwa.com/.

Ford Motor Company. "Henry Ford and Family." http://www.ford.com/en/heritage/fordFamily/default.htm.

Franklin's Flying Circus and Air Show. "Jimmy-Bobby Memorial." http://www.franklinairshow.com/ Memorial.htm.

Goebel, Greg. "The Republic P-47 Thunderbolt." Greg Goebel/In the Public Domain. http://www.vectorsite. net/avp47.html.

Gruner, Ronald H. "The Golden Age of Aviation." Silent Giants. http://www.gruner.com/flight/appendix/ aviators/index.htm.

Hargrave Aviation and Aeromodelling—Interdependent Evolutions and Histories: The Pioneers. "Hilda (Hilde) Beatrice Hewlett (1864–1943)." Monash University. http://www.ctie.monash.edu.au/hargrave/ hewlett.html.

Hawker Beechcraft. http://www.hawkerbeechcraft.com/.

Heavenly Body: North American Aviation B-25J Mitchell Bomber. "The Doolittle Tokyo Raid." http://www.b25.net/pages/dooraid.html.

Henry Ford Museum. "The Wright Brothers." http://www.hfmgv.org/exhibits/wright/.

Herd, Andrew. "Great Airplanes: Ford Trimotor." FlightSim.com. http://www.flightsim.com/cgi/kds?$=main/ feature/trimotor/trimotor.htm.

History Channel. "Amelia Earhart." http://www.thehistorychannel.co.uk/.

Johnson, Bobby H. "Post, Wiley Hardeman." *Handbook of Texas Online*. http://www.tsha.utexas.edu/handbook/ online/articles/PP/fpo27.html.

KCET. "Constellation." Chasing the Sun. PBS. http://www.pbs.org/kcet/chasingthesun/planes/constellation. html.

Koontz, Giacinta Bradley. Harriet Quimby Home Page. http://www.sonictech.net/customers/gia/.

The Library of Congress. "Amelia Earhart." America's Story from America's Library.
    http://www.americaslibrary.gov/cgi-bin/page.cgi/aa/explorers/earhart.

Marshall, Norman S., and Mark J. Denger. "Californians and the Military: General James Harold
    'Jimmy' Doolittle." The California State Military Museum. http://www.militarymuseum.org/Doolittle.
    html.

Martin, J. Cy. "The Forst Smith Aircraft Company and Alexander Airport." http://www.home.flash.net/
    ~cymartin/fsaircc.htm.

Meyer, Jan. "Historical Review." Excerpt from *An Introduction to Deployable Recovery Systems*, Sandia Report
    SAND85-1180 (August 1985). ParachuteHistory.com. http://www.parachutehistory.com/eng/drs.html.

Mid-America Air Museum. "Curtis Wright Pusher." http://www.cityofliberal.com/airmuseum/aircraft/
    production/descriptions/curtiswrightpusher.html.

Millville Army Airfield Museum. "P-47 Thunderbolt." http://www.p47millville.org/P47-Millville.cfm?p=
    P47-Thunderbolt.

Mississippi People. "Roscoe Turner." Northeast Mississippi Community College. http://www2.nemcc.edu/
    mspeople/roscoe_turner.htm.

Museum of Flight. "Aircraft and Spacecraft: Lockheed F-104C Starfighter." http://www.museumofflight.org/
    Collection/Aircraft.asp?RecordKey=98ECEAD8-5B08-4665-8244-63E81D55BC53.

National Aeronautics and Space Administration. http://www.nasa.gov/.

National Aviation Hall of Fame. http://www.nationalaviation.blade6.donet.com/.

National Museum of the United States Air Force. http://www.nationalmuseum.af.mil/.

National Park Service. "Huffman Prairie Flying Field and Interpretive Center." http://www.nps.gov/
    partnerships/huffman_flying_field.htm.

Nielsen, Dale. "Chock to Chock: Where Was I?" Canadian Owners and Pilots Association.
    http://www.copanational.org/non-members/safety/2004/safetyCCJan04.htm.

Pilcher, Walter F. "Hughes, Howard Robard, Jr." *Handbook of Texas Online*.
    http://www.tsha.utexas.edu/handbook/online/articles/HH/fhu60.html.

Royal Air Force Museum. http://www.rafmuseum.org.uk/.

Royal Canadian Air Force. "Ford Trimotor." http://www.rcaf.com/aircraft/transports/trimotor/index.
    php?name=Trimotor.

Schamel, John. "The Development of Night Navigation in the U.S." Federal Aviation Administration Air Traffic
    Division: Flight Service History. http://www.atctraining.faa.gov/afss/History/nightnav.htm.

Shanaberger, Kenneth W. "Wright J-6 Whirlwind." KensAviation.com. http://www.shanaberger.com/engines/
    R-975.htm.

Smithsonian National Air and Space Museum. http://www.nasm.si.edu/.

Smithsonian National Postal Museum. http://www.postalmuseum.si.edu/.

Society of Air Racing Historians. http://www.airrace.com/.

Stock, Marvin E. "History of the 450th Bombardment Group (H)." Official Home of the 450th BG Association. http://www.450thbg.com/real/biographies/stock/stock.shtml.

Stuber, Irene. "Bentonville Woman Boldly Flew as No Woman Had Flown Before." Women of Achievement and Herstory. The Liz Library. http://www.thelizlibrary.org/undelete/woa-spotlight/01-thaden.html.

Taylorcraft Foundation. "Taylorcraft Corporation and Armour and Co." Transcript of original radio broadcast on WFAH (Alliance, Ohio), November 19, 1956. http://www.taylorcraft.org/docs/taylorcraft_wfah_1956.pdf.

Thompson, D. C., and John Hanks. "Guide to Transportation History Resources." 1999. Revised by William Hopkins, 2003. University of Wyoming American Heritage Center. http://www.ahc.uwyo.edu/documents/use_archives/guides/transportation%20columnhighres.pdf.

Todd, Gail. "Art Initiative Will Save Indy Airport from Terminal Dullness." *Red Orbit*, February 21, 2006. http://www.redorbit.com/.

United States Air Force. "Fact Sheet: B-25J Mitchell." http://www2.hurlburt.af.mil/library/factsheets/factsheet.asp?id=3424.

United States Centennial of Flight Commission. http://www.centennialofflight.gov/.

United States Department of Transportation. "Federal Aviation Administration Advisory Circular AC 61-67b: Stall and Spin Awareness Training." May 17, 1991. http://www.atlasaviation.com/AviationLibrary/StallandSpinAwareness/Stall_And_Spin_Awareness.htm.

United States Parachute Association. "The Sport of Skydiving: Skydiving History." Reproduced from Dan Poynter and Mike Turoff's *Parachuting: The Skydiver's Handbook*. Santa Barbara, CA: Para Publishing, 2000. http://www.uspa.org/about/sport.htm.

Virtual Aircraft Museum. "Driggs Aircraft Corporation." http://avia.russian.ee/manufacturers/0746.html.

Virtual Aviation Museum. "Kategorie Reconnaissance until 1913." http://luftfahrtmuseum.com/htmi/itk/a1.htm.

WGBH Educational Foundation. "Last Flight of Bomber 31." NOVA. PBS. http://www.pbs.org/wgbh/nova/bomber/.

Wilbur Wright Birthplace and Museum. http://www.wwbirthplace.com/.

Wings over Kansas. "Aviation History." http://www.wingsoverkansas.com/history/.

Wright Brothers Aeroplane Company and Museum of Pioneer Aviation. "Tale of the Vin Fiz." http://www.first-to-fly.com/History/History%20of%20Airplane/vinfiztale.htm.

Index